MOJANG

MINECRAFT™

MOBESTIARY

ONLINE SAFETY FOR YOUNGER FANS

Spending time online is great fun! Here are a few simple rules to help younger fans stay safe and keep the Internet a great place to spend time:
- Never give out your real name—don't use it as your username.
- Never give out any of your personal details.
- Never tell anybody which school you go to or how old you are.
- Never tell anybody your password except a parent or a guardian.
- Be aware that you must be 13 or over to create an account on many sites. Always check the site policy and ask a parent or guardian for permission before registering.
- Always tell a parent or guardian if something is worrying you.

Published in the United States by Del Rey, an imprint of Random House, a division of Penguin Random House LLC, New York.

DEL REY and the HOUSE colophon are registered trademarks of Penguin Random House LLC.

Published in hardcover in the United Kingdom by Egmont UK Limited.

ISBN 978-1-5247-9716-4
Ebook ISBN 978-1-5247-9744-7

Printed in China on acid-free paper by RRD Asia Printing Solutions

Written by Alex Wiltshire
Additional material by Stephanie Milton and Marsh Davies

Illustrated by Anton Stenvall

Special thanks to Lydia Winters, Owen Jones, Junkboy,
Martin Johansson, Marsh Davies and Ryan Marsh

randomhousebooks.com

2 4 6 8 9 7 5 3

First U. S. Edition

Design by Andrea Philpots

MOJANG

MINECRAFT™

MOBESTIARY

DEL REY • NEW YORK

CONTENTS

PREFACE

As I sit here in my warm study, surrounded by my treasured books, my mind turns to the worlds beyond my windows. Out there, countless adventurers are courageously exploring the Overworld and beyond. They are trekking across deep forests and dry deserts; they are digging far below the surface of the land and building up into the clouds.

The worlds they travel are filled with great wonder. As an explorer myself, I have seen places where spikes of ice claw at the sky, and where mesas striped with many colors crowd the horizon.

I have also faced many terrible dangers. There are few places which are safe from hostile mobs. These awful creatures wish ill on all who wander near. Some are appalling even to imagine, and quite turn my stomach. But while they so often present mortal threat, they are also often the source of many items and treasures which all adventurers prize.

Not all creatures have evil intent. There are passive and tameable mobs which provide one with sustenance, hardworking labor and heartwarming companionship. They make life in the wilderness not only possible but also tolerable.

Through all my exploration of the worlds, I have amassed countless records, accounts and descriptions of every creature which walks, stalks, flies or burrows in the Overworld, Nether and End. Through the observations and research of other great explorers and scientists, I have been able to supplement my findings with additional knowledge about these beasts, and have decided that it is time to pass on this knowledge to you.

This encyclopedia, or, as I call it, Mobestiary, contains information on the habits, habitats and hallmarks of every mob which has so far been discovered, alongside my illustrations of their appearance. I wish you to use it to arm yourself against the perils you will face on your journeys. From the smallest endermite to the hugest wither, the softest rabbit to the friendliest golem, identifying mobs and understanding where they live and how they behave is of incalculable value.

The time has come for me to retire from my role as explorer, and so I leave you with my life's work – a thorough account of every mob discovered so far in this strange and perilous world. I therefore wish you all the very best. I shall be thinking of you, here in the safety of my study, as my book helps you achieve the highest glories.

The Naturalist

PASSIVE MOBS

◆

Let us first study the passive mobs that roam the Overworld. From the cave-dwelling bat to the water-loving squid, you will find these gentle creatures are often the source of many useful items, including meat to sustain an adventurer's health.

Fig. I.

Field sketch of a pair of bats in flight.

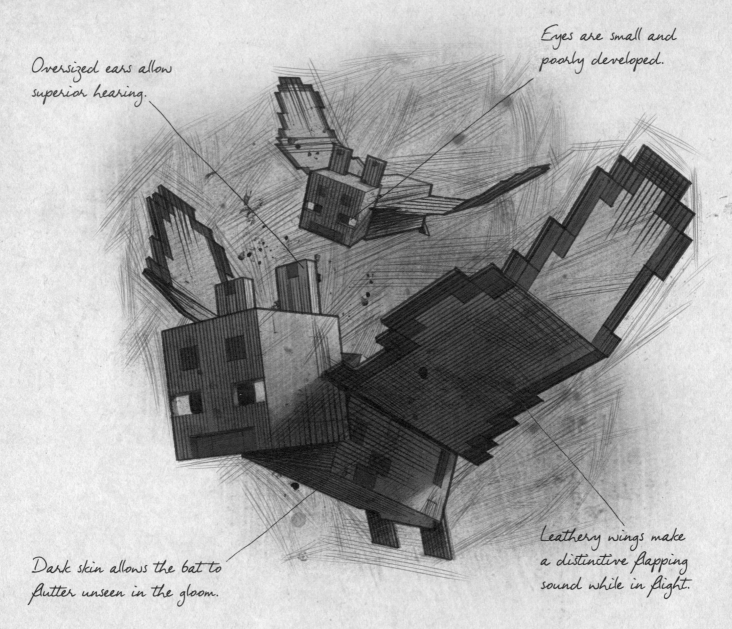

Oversized ears allow superior hearing.

Eyes are small and poorly developed.

Dark skin allows the bat to flutter unseen in the gloom.

Leathery wings make a distinctive flapping sound while in flight.

BAT

One might be inclined to think the bat a sinister creature of the dark, with its leathery wings, blood-sucking tendencies and evil intentions. But research has proven this to be an unfair image of bats. In fact, they are quite harmless and shy of explorers. Indeed, it is better to think of them as flying mice, squeaking as they flutter through caves, navigating by echolocation.

THE CAVERN DWELLER

Bats live in the darkest places of the world, at ground level or deeper, and can often be found roosting in caves on the underside of blocks such as stone. They are easily startled, however. At the merest sight of any adventurer, they will take flight in fear. The poor creature often finds itself unable to get away and forced to flap toward the adventurer who frightened it.

This blind panic is often misunderstood as destructive intent. In fact, I have witnessed some particularly unlucky bats flying into lava, catching on fire and desperately flapping about, squeaking pathetically until their sad and inevitable demise.

Bats are fairly weak creatures, and they will die with just a single strike of an iron sword or a fully drawn-back arrow. But we must be gentle with these tiny fellows, for they drop no item when they die. Mind you, their erratic flight and minute size make them surprisingly difficult to hit, but please do not think this makes these furry innocents a fine source of target practice. There are plenty of other, truly evil creatures roaming the worlds to try one's skills upon.

CONTROL OF BATS

Many explorers, including myself, have come to treasure the gentle company of bats which have chosen to live in their houses. But after spending time exploring lands far from home and then returning, they've often found their friends missing. It seems that bats will come and go as they please.

If one is lucky enough to find a name tag in a dungeon chest or to find such an item available to trade from a villager, then one can use it to give one's favorite bat a name by first renaming the tag with an anvil, and then using the tag on the creature. A named bat, like any named mob, will never disappear, unless it is killed.

Some explorers find, to their irritation, that bats appear in spaces where they are not welcome. A roosting bat would not be appreciated in a fancy house, for example. In such cases the best course of prevention is to keep the ceilings of one's house brightly lit at all times so bats have nowhere they feel comfortable to settle. (One may argue that any truly fancy house will be naturally bat-proof, since it will be brightly lit as a matter of course.)

BRAVER AND BOLDER

There are certain times in the year when bats become more daring and venture into brighter places than usual. Accounts vary but they seem to fall between the dates of October 20 and November 3, when the nights draw in, and some fancy that ghouls and witches roam across the land.

Bats seem to prefer enclosed, dark places to the perils of open land, however. Some adventurers have discovered a rather clever use for this tendency, employing bats as guides to the location of secret chambers. If you can hear their squeaks on the other side of walls or beneath your feet, you'll know there must be a dark space hidden nearby. Carefully follow the sound and you should find it. But beware the presence of mobs of the dark which are less gentle.

CHICKEN

The chicken can be found wandering any grassy biome in the Overworld. Fearless of adventurers like us, chickens are friendly unless they are attacked, whereupon they break into feathery alarm and try to get away. But since they are flightless, they rarely get very far. The chicken has many uses so settlers should consider taking them into their homestead.

USE OF EGGS

Many explorers are more than happy to slaughter chickens for their succulent meat, which, when cooked in a furnace, smells and tastes quite delicious. Please be cautious: one must never try to eat chicken without cooking it first. Raw chicken is not only less filling, but also has a chance of inflicting one with food poisoning. Should one experience this unhappy condition, one will find oneself becoming more hungry for a period. Without enough healthy food to keep one's strength up, severe sickness is sure to follow.

But one need not kill chickens in order to obtain food. An adult bird will lay an egg every five to ten minutes.

Eggs cannot be eaten directly (I once tried this, and suffered unhappy results), but they have two special uses. First, one can cook with them. Combine an egg with three milk, two sugar and three wheat to make moist and delicious cake. Cake bakes into a special block which can be sliced into seven pieces. Or combine an egg with one pumpkin and sugar to make pumpkin pie, which

is very filling. Second, one can throw eggs. They don't deal damage to mobs or other explorers, but will push them backward. This is a somewhat useful tactic in a pinch, since it will keep your opponents at bay, but is otherwise a rather fruitless exercise. If, however, one were to throw an egg at the ground, there's a one in eight chance that from it a chick will hatch.

BREEDING CHICKENS

Throwing eggs is thus an excellent way to produce a large flock of chickens. But there is another way to breed them. Feed a pair of adult birds wheat seeds and they'll produce a chick.

Chicks grow into maturity in twenty minutes, or faster if you feed them seeds. Chicks will delightfully follow adult chickens wherever they go, but all chickens will follow you if seeds are held near them, which presents an efficient way of herding them into a fenced enclosure.

It is recommended that you keep chickens in such fenced enclosures to help ensure they're not attacked by their

main wild predator, the fierce ocelot. But even if a chicken is inside a fenced area, an ocelot can reach through the fence and attack if the chicken is close enough to the edge, so one must be careful not to overcrowd them and ensure they have plenty of space.

There is one other reason why one might choose to breed chickens: their feathers, which are dropped when they die, are an important component for crafting arrows for one's bow.

THE CHICKEN SPY

Some explorers have noticed that wherever there are evil mobs, a chicken always seems to be quietly watching, leading them to suspect that the chicken is some sort of spy for the dark forces.

Could this theory have anything to do with confusion over the chicken jockey, that rare phenomenon of the baby zombie, or zombie pigman, riding a chicken? Or perhaps there really is more than meets the eye to the chicken? I hope that continued studies will soon answer this conundrum.

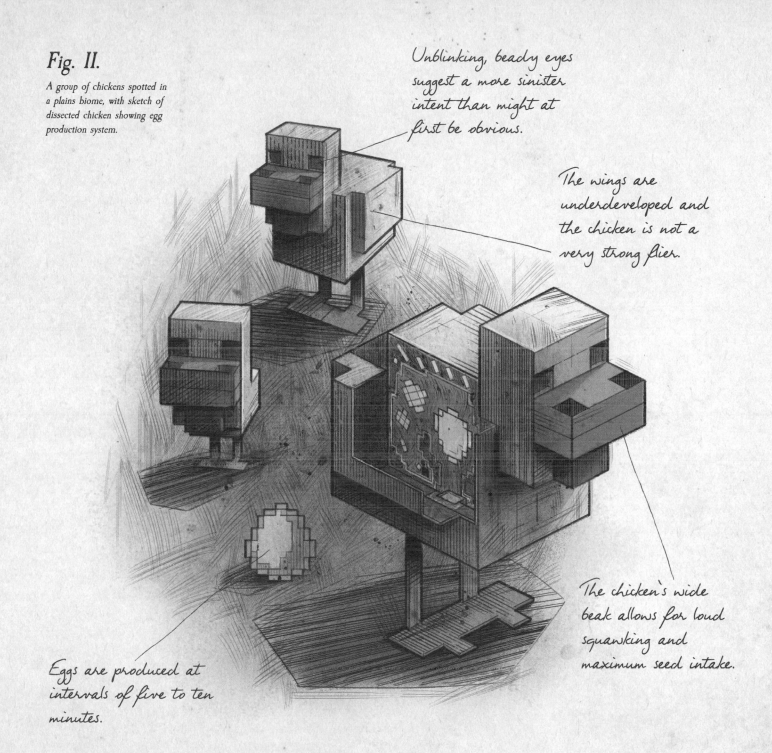

Fig. II.

A group of chickens spotted in a plains biome, with sketch of dissected chicken showing egg production system.

Unblinking, beady eyes suggest a more sinister intent than might at first be obvious.

The wings are underdeveloped and the chicken is not a very strong flier.

The chicken's wide beak allows for loud squawking and maximum seed intake.

Eggs are produced at intervals of five to ten minutes.

Fig. III.

A happy family of cows with newborn calf.

The hide is fairly tough – cows drop leather which can be crafted into several useful items.

A large mouth and nose result in heavy breathing and deep mooing.

Long legs allow for hasty escape from potential dangers.

Sizeable loins make the cow an excellent source of steak.

COW

This docile mammal can be found wherever in the Overworld there is grass, often in herds of four animals. They moo and snort, and potter from block to block with little evident sense, but are very useful to adventurers. Whether one is in need of basic armor, a full belly, relief from terrible afflictions, or simply wishes to decorate one's home, the cow can provide.

MILK AND STEAK

Cows drop between one and three pieces of raw beef, which becomes steak when cooked in a furnace. Hot beef, cooked rare so the juices run from it, is a wonderful dish, but this nourishing meal is also worthy of filling any backpack or chest, since cold steak is a delightful dish, too. Like all meat, beef – whether cooked or raw – may be fed to wolves to restore their health and will induce them into breeding.

Cows also yield a very special substance of which all explorers should be aware – milk doesn't fill one's belly but it has the rather wonderful capacity to remove any strange effects on one's body. If one finds oneself poisoned by a cave spider or slowed by a witch, milk will instantly cure all effects. But one must be aware, however, that milk will cancel out both bad and good effects, so if you've just consumed a good potion of invisibility or fire resistance, you might not wish to remove it.

To obtain milk, simply use an empty bucket on a cow. All wise adventurers take this wholesome elixir wherever they go, but it will take up a good deal of space in one's pack, since the buckets do not stack.

USES OF LEATHER

Cows also provide tough yet soft leather. Each beast can drop up to two pieces, ready to be fashioned into jackets, leggings, boots and hats. Leather armor is rather less protective than armor made of iron, but some find its style more to their liking.

Leather may also be crafted into the backing of item frames and is used for the binding of books. The former is excellent for decorating one's house to give it a homely appearance, and books are essential for anyone who wishes to dabble in enchantments, as well as any lover of learning in general.

Some researchers have heard tell of two legendary titles being granted to those adventurers who work with cows. The first time one takes leather dropped from a cow, one gains the title Cow Tipper, and the first time one breeds a cow, one becomes branded with the title Repopulation.

BREEDING COWS

One cannot amass a herd of cows as quickly as one can gain a flock of chickens, for cows are unfortunately not known to be able to lay eggs. Instead, two cows must be fed wheat so that they are induced into breeding. The pressures and strains of calf-rearing are such that it will take five minutes until the parents are ready to breed again.

The calf will mature to adulthood in twenty minutes, so a full day, from sunrise to sunrise. But, if one is in a hurry, one can speed their growth by feeding them with more wheat. Each sheaf will reduce the remaining time for a calf to fully grow by a tenth. Those intent on producing a big herd, or intent on building up their stocks of beef or milk, would do well to note this, since baby animals do not drop anything, cannot be milked, and cannot breed with other cows.

Curiously, all specimens have both udders and horns, and yet may pair to produce offspring. This observation hasn't yet been fully explained.

MOOSHROOM

Some years ago, far-flung explorers discovered a rare and fantastical biome called the mushroom island. They reported that it was inhabited by strange red and black cows covered in mushrooms. The mooshroom, as it has come to be named, is an odd subspecies of cow which is found in herds of four, and only on the mycelium blocks of mushroom islands.

MUSHROOM CUISINE

The mooshroom's close kinship with the cow is demonstrated by the fact that raw beef drops from specimens when they are killed. Whether cooked into steak or eaten raw, it tastes just like the real thing, despite some enthusiasts claiming it is more flavorful. The animal may also be milked with a bucket, just as one might milk a cow.

However, if one were to "milk" a mooshroom with a bowl rather than a bucket, one will find the bowl full of wonderfully hearty mushroom stew. This dish is usually cooked with red and brown mushrooms, and is very nourishing indeed. A single mooshroom can supply an endless amount of the stuff; one's only limit is how many bowls one has, and how much space one has to store them.

TRANSFORMATION

Now, current scientific thinking is that the mooshroom's diet of mycelium has either led to some kind of symbiotic relationship between the cow and the fungus, or that it might be some kind of infection. Whichever is the case, it seems to lead to yet another interesting property. If one shears a mooshroom, five red mushrooms will fall from its hide, and the beast will transform with a puff of smoke into a regular cow. This cow behaves and looks just like any cow; it can even be bred with other cows, and cannot breed with mooshrooms. Even mooshroom calves forget these beasts are their parents.

The academic world was quite stunned when it witnessed this remarkable behavior, which has never been seen before. Theories abound in attempting to explain it, but while most scholars do not quite understand the process, it is generally agreed that the act of shearing somehow entirely removes the fungus from the mooshroom's body, and thereby returns it to its natural condition. Quite astonishing.

BREEDING MOOSHROOMS

Since it is such a rich source of fine food, many adventurers find that the mooshroom is a valuable addition to their livestock. It is therefore strongly advised that they are not sheared, and are instead allowed to maintain their special qualities. Breeding them is quite simple. Just as with cows, one must use wheat on two adult mooshrooms, and from their union will come a calf. Calves, like cows, will take a full day and night to grow to maturity, and will not drop any item, yield experience or be able to breed until they have done so. It is possible, however, to accelerate their development by feeding them wheat.

Since they can only be found in the rare mushroom island biomes, mooshrooms are likely to be far from most adventurers' homesteads. Once mooshrooms have been located, they can be led by standing nearby and holding a handful of wheat, but the resulting journey is sure to be most difficult. Some adventurers have tried introducing mooshrooms to their farms by taking mycelium from a mushroom island biome and planting it on their land, but their experiments have failed to produce any mooshrooms. Some then found their entire farms overtaken by the peculiar stuff, and found nothing but mushrooms would grow.

Fig. IV.

A family of grazing mooshrooms, with dissected view to show the mooshroom's milk and mushroom soup production systems.

Milk and mushroom soup production systems are located toward bottom rear of mooshroom.

Mushroom growth across back appears to cause the creature no discomfort.

The mooshroom has the same long legs and fleshy loins as the cow.

Fig. V.

Field sketch of a family of pigs.

A large, flat nose aids the pig's keen sense of smell — essential to sniff out sources of food.

Of stocky build due to its healthy appetite, the pig is an excellent source of pork.

Four short legs — the pig is no speedy beast.

PIG

The pig might seem a simple soul, wandering the Overworld much like any cow or sheep. Yet further study of this common pink porcine has revealed some interesting attributes that merit discussion. Simply by holding a carrot, beetroot or potato before a pig, one can lead it around, a behavior that makes this beast quite simple to manage and farm.

KEEPING PIGS

Pigs are valuable animals due to the raw porkchops they drop when they die. Each pig will drop up to three chops, and they're a fine source of food indeed when they are cooked. As with other creatures which drop their meat, a pig will drop cooked porkchops if it is killed by fire. An efficient way to collect cooked meat, therefore, is to set fire to a large group of animals, but perhaps this is cruel...

If you wish to breed pigs it is a simple matter of feeding two pigs carrots, beetroots or potatoes when they are near each other, to induce them into the process. Once induced, it won't be long before a baby pig appears between the two adults. It will take a full day for this little hog to grow to its full adult size, and during this time it will remain close to its parents. Until it is full-grown, it will not drop any meat and cannot be bred with other pigs. I have discovered that feeding the baby pig a carrot, beetroot or potato will speed its development, taking away approximately a tenth of its remaining time to grow. Farming pigs is all very well, but these chubby mammals have rather more remarkable features besides, which we shall now investigate.

RIDING THE PIG

Pigs may be ridden if one has a saddle. Only adventurers of the highest caliber can become pig-riders, since saddles cannot be crafted, and must be found in chests in such places as dungeons, Nether fortresses and temples.

The earliest pig riders found they had no control over where the pig would go, but they soon designed a clever steering implement which takes advantage of the pig's innate greed. Called a carrot on a stick and made with a fishing rod and carrot, it dangles a delicious treat before the pig's nose. The pig can be led in the desired direction since it will eagerly trot after the carrot. The pig is so eager, in fact, that it may easily be steered into tumbling from a cliff. The poor animal will break its rider's fall, but die in the process.

A pig does not travel particularly quickly, but it can be encouraged to put on a surprising burst of speed by allowing it a bite of the carrot, whereupon it will double its normal trotting speed for forty seconds. Each carrot and stick lasts for about three bites, after which it will have been fully consumed and will boost the pig no more.

LEGENDS OF PIGS

One legend tells of a humanoid and intelligent race of pigs which lived in the Overworld at one time. No such creatures can be found today, and yet we must consider the existence of the zombie pigman. Some scholars suggest that pigs are the descendants of this older race and that proof lies in the fact that if a pig is struck by lightning it will transform into a zombie pigman. This is compelling evidence, but our studies continue.

There is another interesting legend which tells of the pig's creation, and how a godly experiment went badly wrong, resulting in the awful creeper coming into existence. If you compare these two creatures today, it is hard to imagine how this absurd story came to be, but there are some who swear it has roots in the truth.

RABBIT

Travelers will often encounter rabbits across savannas, deep forests, taiga and swamps. They come in several varieties, distinguished by their golden, spotted, white, brown or black fur. Rabbits seem highly aware of their surroundings. Indeed, their keen vision allows them to perceive both threats and sources of food at great distances.

USES OF RABBITS

Various scholars argue that the rabbit's love for carrots can be a problem for vegetable farmers. Unless they wish to see their crops plucked from the earth and consumed by these voracious mammals, they must enclose them within sturdy fences.

Rabbits may be small, but their bodies yield several useful items when they die. Four of their hides may be combined into leather, and when cooked, their meat is a good source of food. But it is far more nourishing when cooked into stew with a bowl, mushroom, carrot and baked potato.

On rare occasions, rabbits have been discovered to drop a rabbit's foot. This is a lucky find indeed, for the rabbit's foot may be brewed with an awkward potion to create a potion of leaping. In its basic form, this concoction does not provide much extra height, but several explorers have told tales in which it aided them as they fell from a precipice, because this potion also reduces falling damage. On brewing the potion with glowstone dust, however, one will discover a stronger infusion which allows one to clear a full two blocks in a single bound.

BREEDING RABBITS

Through experimentation I discovered that rabbits may be induced to breed by feeding two adults carrots or dandelions. Their offspring will tend to inherit the coloring of its parent, before steadily growing to adulthood. It is possible to accelerate their development by feeding them further carrots.

Prospective rabbit ranchers should be aware of the rabbit's mortal enemy, the wolf. Wolves will attack rabbits on sight, causing them to scatter, emitting pitiable squeaks of pain as they are bitten. Even a tamed wolf, which will not attack rabbits on account of its training, will throw them into a panic.

THE KILLER BUNNY

Voyagers of the Overworld have brought back tales of a terrifying phenomenon that disproves the commonly held belief that all rabbits are gentle. They say that in exceedingly rare cases a rabbit will turn out bad. The killer bunny, as it has been called, may be identified by its white fur, narrowed red eyes, and ferocious temperament, which it unleashes upon people and wolves alike. Its heightened senses enable it to locate its victims from great distance. It can then close in on them in an instant, for it bounds far faster than any normal rabbit.

The killer bunny strikes with great savagery, hitting harder than an enderman. Those who have faced one and lived tell tales of its cunning tricks in combat. It will leap away, persuading you to believe you have it on the run, only to turn and redouble its assault. Many travelers have fallen prey to this cruel tactic from this most unlikely of foes.

Some chroniclers have suggested that the killer bunny was once immortalized in a popular comedic play, in which it torments the warriors of a great king and causes much death and everyone's shameful retreat. It is, apparently, an amusing entertainment.

Fig. VI.

A herd of rabbits.
Note the killer bunny
on the left.

The rabbit's delicate button-nose is capable of picking up the scent of carrots from some distance.

The killer bunny's eyes are narrowed with hatred.

The muted color of the rabbit's coat allows it to blend into the natural landscape.

Fig. VII.

A herd of humble sheep, one of which has recently been sheared.

A dense cloud of wool covers the head and body and keeps the sheep warm.

Facial expression suggests the sheep is slow-witted and gentle.

Sheep's head, and therefore brain, are relatively small.

SHEEP

These meek creatures commonly flock in fours wherever grass can be found naturally growing. Like many passive mobs, the sheep is an excellent farm animal, though one must be careful that hungry wolves do not get near them. As well as providing soft and warm wool, sheep also drop raw mutton, which can be cooked into a delicious, if somewhat chewy, meal.

GATHERING WOOL

One of the sheep's greatest benefits is its wool production. This textile is a useful resource, for it is required to make a bed – a most important item for all explorers. Wool is also indispensable for making all manner of homely items, such as carpet, paintings and banners.

There are two methods of collecting wool. First, sheep will often drop a single block of wool when you kill them. A more efficient way to collect wool is to use shears, a tool crafted with two iron ingots. By using them on a sheep, its wool will be clipped, an entirely harmless operation which leaves the sheep bald, but garners you between one and three blocks. The sheep's wool will regrow when it has eaten grass, and will be ready to be sheared again. By allowing them land to roam, sheep will enjoy a good supply of grass and soon grow a new coat.

COLORS OF WOOL

Not all sheep wool is alike. One in five sheep does not wear a white wool coat, but one of several natural colors.

Scholars have recorded light and dark gray, black, brown and, rarest of all, pink. The pink sheep is a one in a thousand marvel that any true sheep enthusiast wishes to see, and its wool is highly treasured.

But those wishing for even more outlandish colors of wool need not be disappointed. I discovered that one can dye sheep with any of the 16 different pigments known to science, and then shear them to achieve the tone of wool one desires. These dyed sheep regrow their wool in the same color, so one only needs one dose of dye to shear as much wool as the sheep can produce.

BREEDING SHEEP

Like other passive mobs, sheep are easily bred. Despite the sheep's love of grass, one must feed them wheat to encourage a pair to make a lamb. The lamb will grow into adulthood in about a day, but its growth can be speeded by feeding it more wheat. Until it is fully grown, a sheep cannot be sheared, will not drop mutton, but it will feed on grass voraciously, even faster than its parents.

Dye isn't the only way to create new shades of wool – a more natural alternative exists. It may also be achieved by breeding two sheep of different colors. Their lamb will be a mixture of both hues. Thus, if a red sheep breeds with a yellow one, their lamb will be orange. A blue and a white pairing of sheep will create a light blue offspring, and so it goes on. If a lamb's parents are of colors which do not have a natural, logical result when mixed, the lamb will take the color of just one of them.

A final word. If one were to give one's favorite woolly beast a mystical name it will gain a fantastical multicolored coat of wool. The wool color will cycle through the 16 known pigments in turn, repeatedly, transforming the sheep into a fascinating curiosity. These runes must be inscribed upon a name tag with an anvil: "jeb_." Unfortunately, its wool does not retain this magical color-shifting property when sheared. Great studies have gone into uncovering the name's mystery, and it is currently thought that it refers to an all-powerful god.

SQUID

Many residents of the Overworld feel rather repulsed by this ocean dweller, but the truth is that the squid is entirely harmless. Found splashing at or near the surface of any body of water, the squid does not attack people and will merely attempt to swim away if it should be attacked itself. The squid is, in fact, the prey of far worse horrors that live in the sea.

HABITS OF THE SQUID

In olden times, adventurers would tell rip-roaring yarns in which seamen coursing the open ocean crashed their boats into squid and found their vessels instantly destroyed. Today, this does not happen. Perhaps the boats of old were far more fragile than our own, but one can happily set forth on the sea and never need to worry that they might be spilled into it by the rubbery bodies of these water-dwelling mollusks.

Nevertheless, squid are strong, if rather directionless, swimmers. They appear to use their eight tentacles to propel themselves, swelling them open and then tightening and closing them, essentially pushing themselves head-first through the water. It does not seem so when described in this way, but it is actually a rather graceful technique of locomotion and it gives them the ability to progress surprisingly easily against strong water currents.

Despite their size, squid can survive in a single block of water, their tentacles trailing over the land around their pool. One cannot imagine that they are particularly happy to be confined in such a small space, but they will survive the ordeal nonetheless.

INK DROPS

The squid does not drop its meat, but it is the source of a substance which allows one to dye things black. When a squid is killed, it will drop between one and three ink sacs, which may be applied to any stainable item. For example, using an ink sac on a sheep will make its wool black, and combining an ink sac with clay will create black hardened clay. Or it can be crafted into a black firework star with gunpowder and a feather, and, indeed, other specific items such as gold nuggets or mob heads to produce different explosive effects.

Squid use this ink in a mysterious fashion. Travelers of some worlds have reported that in their lands squid will eject a cloud of the stuff when they are attacked, presumably as a way of covering their escape, but this behavior has yet to be observed in the larger worlds. Indeed, these miniature alternative worlds hold another surprise: only there can squid be found with babies. In no domain, however, are they known to breed.

PREDATORS OF THE SQUID

The squid's natural foes are the guardian and elder guardian which will attack the poor squid on sight, killing them in just two blasts of their awful beam attack. Squid may be part of their natural diet, or they may simply hate anything and everything that wanders close to their ocean monuments.

A squid's secondary foe is the air. When beached on land, a squid is unable to move other than to pulse its tentacles. It may only survive for a few seconds before expiring. It is thought that the speed of their death on land is partly due to the tendency of their soft bodies to dry out in the air, and partly because their soft bodies cannot support their internal organs without water to buoy them. Their own weight crushes them. To see the squid so vulnerable reminds one of how little reason there is to hate this peculiar organism.

Fig. VIII.
Dissected squid with brain and ink production system clearly visible.

The squid's bulbous form contains a swollen ink sac which it drops upon death.

Dark blue skin makes squid difficult to spot in the murky depths.

The squid is harmless and never uses its teeth as weapons.

Fig. IX.
Underside of squid showing large mouth and teeth.

Eight legs undulate as the squid propels itself through water.

Fig. X.

A brown-robed farmer
sketched during a visit to my
nearest NPC village.

A large, beaky nose
gives a nasal, honking
quality to the
villager's voice.

Villagers' skulls contain
sizable brains which
they put to good use
calculating trade deals.

The arms always seem
to be folded across the
body – a defensive
posture, perhaps.

Robes appear to vary
depending on the
villager's profession.

VILLAGER

When traveling across deserts and plains, one will come across settlements of people known as villagers. They are similar to us and perform many functions of a civilized society. We can trade with them and seek their shelter in times of need. They ply varied trades, retire to their homes when darkness falls, and run from the dangers of the world.

VILLAGER BABIES
Villagers will come together to produce offspring. Their babies are endearing fellows, and can often be spotted chasing after each other. They also display much curiosity toward iron golems, which many larger villages, with populations of at least ten, will have as a resident. And, most charmingly, if an iron golem is holding a poppy, a baby villager will gently take it.

While we can put chickens and cows into a breeding state, villagers do things their own way, producing babies with regard to the number of doors in their village. Adventurers may therefore boost a village's population by raising the number of doors in it. Do ensure that these doors lead inside a building, and do not simply stand outside. Villagers are not so easily fooled.

THREATS TO LIFE
The life of a villager can be brutal and short. I know from experience that even the weather can be a threat to their well-being. If the nearby ground around a villager is struck by lightning, it will transform into a rather nasty witch.

But a villager's mortal enemies are the zombie and zombie pigman. By night, those beasts will mercilessly hunt villagers down, even breaking through their doors. If they are caught, the zombies will kill them, or transform them into zombie villagers. The villagers have no personal defense, instead looking to their sturdy iron golems to aid them, or, indeed, passing travelers such as you or I.

To cure a zombie villager, one must cause them weakness with a splash potion, and then feed them a golden apple. Over the course of several minutes they will turn back to normal.

TERMS OF TRADING
Villagers take different professions, as indicated by the color of their robes. Farmers, fishers, shepherds and fletchers wear brown; librarians wear white. Clerics, a kind of priest, wear purple robes; armorers, weaponsmiths and toolsmiths wear black aprons; butchers and leatherworkers wear white aprons. As one might expect, villagers trade the items that are connected to their profession.

For example, clerics will trade in enchanted items and ender pearls, while librarians prefer to trade in books and compasses.

Villagers value emeralds above all, whether they use them as currency or sell items in return for emeralds. But not all are trustworthy, so be wary of being cheated. Sometimes they might stock items which are very hard to come across in the Overworld; for these, the value might be sizable.

Once one has traded with a villager, they begin to trust you as a client and will offer an extra trade. With more transactions, they will continue to add trades up to a maximum of five, but will only trade the same offer three to five times before they grow tired of it. Keep them happier by varying trades.

Since emeralds are rarely located in the ground, villagers are a valuable source. If one can find a farmer willing to trade them in return for something easy to farm, one can quickly make a small fortune.

NEUTRAL MOBS

These complex creatures may be passive or hostile, depending on the circumstances. It has been necessary to study their behavior most carefully in order to determine what angers them.

Fig. XI.

Two cave spiders poised to attack in the corridors of an abandoned mineshaft.

Blue skin is infused with a potent poison.

Glowing red eyes see all, even in darkness.

Eight hairy legs allow it to cling to walls and spring over obstacles. It scuttles faster than its larger cousin.

Needle-like fangs drip a terrible and fast-acting poison.

CAVE SPIDER

Deep underground lives a dangerous relative of the common spider. Smaller of body, the cave spider lives in abandoned mineshafts and is distinguished by its blue-black hue. In other ways they are identical to their cousin – they are quick and agile and also become docile in bright conditions. So why are cave spiders thought to be so dangerous? Well, they are poisonous.

A VENOMOUS THREAT

The cave spider delivers poison to its victim through its bites. Careful experiments have been performed and the results have shown that when this awful arachnid sinks its fangs into the flesh of its victims, it attempts to inject its venom into the wound through a hole in each fang tip. The bite itself deals a degree of damage, but for those afflicted, it is merely the start of a period of considerable pain. Victims will lose a little of their health every second or so, regardless of the sturdiness of their armor. How long this poor victim will take to recover depends on the level of danger present in their world, but usually they can expect a recovery after either seven or fifteen seconds, which can be quite enough to bring them close to death.

To be quite clear, the cave spider's poison will only reduce health as far as half a heart, and no further. Thus, those who already have very low health are immune to poison, but all victims of cave spiders find themselves dreadfully exposed to mortal blows, including bites from the cave spider itself. The best remedy for explorers of abandoned mineshafts is cow's milk. Carry lots of it, for a single dose will clear the body of the effects of poisoning.

CAVE SPIDER HABITAT

The tight corridors of abandoned mineshafts give an adventurer few opportunities to escape the cave spider's deadly leap. Worse, the cave spider also tends to fill these corridors with its webs. Like the common spider, it is able to scuttle through its webs unimpeded, while anything else, whether mob or brave adventurer, becomes helplessly tangled in their sticky threads, finding their movement slowed almost to nothing as they are exposed to the cave spider's dripping mandibles.

It is all too common to find these beasts in dense clusters. They emerge from spawners in sufficiently gloomy light, and thus, many explorers have told stories of blundering into rooms overflowing with cave spiders and finding themselves swarmed. They jump at any unfortunate visitors, delivering poisonous bites and chasing them down the corridors of the mineshaft.

DEALING WITH SPAWNERS

There are various tactical approaches for dealing with spawners. Some clever explorers like to mine their way above the spawner's location, and then tip lava over it, killing any spiders nearby and making it so bright in the room that no more can spawn. This technique is effective against many types of spawner. (But do not forget that it is rather less useful against a blaze.)

Others suggest digging under the spawner, and destroying it from below, or building a wall with a single-block hole through which the spawner can be reached and destroyed. Still, one must be cautious with facing cave spiders this way, since their small body allows them to fit through a single-block gap. One can also employ a bucket of water when approaching a cave spider spawner, using a flood to wash its webs away. Lighting the area around the spawner is strongly advised, since it will prevent more of these disagreeable creatures from arriving. Be cautious indeed of this destructive crawler.

ENDERMAN

It is strange to think that Overworld inhabitants are host to visitors not of our world. We have called these creatures the endermen and they are altogether alien. Sometimes they seem almost playful, and at other times they attack without mercy. Endermen seem highly intelligent, and appear to worship the ender dragon, but no one has ever successfully communicated with them.

ENDERMEN ORIGINS

The enderman comes from the End. Curiously, these beings do not appear to live in the towers of the recently discovered End cities, preferring to wander the open ground. I have not yet discovered exactly how they travel to our worlds, or why, but as far as I can tell they visit by night, and seem to return to their home by day.

It is also clear that endermen use ender pearls to teleport in order to escape such discomfort as rain (water appears to be a form of poison to an enderman), or to dodge such peril as arrows. An enderman will often drop its pearl when killed. When thrown, a pearl will cause its thrower to be instantly transported to the location it has fallen, consuming the pearl and causing small injury. Combined with a blaze rod, a pearl creates an eye of ender, which is used to build a portal to the End.

HABITS OF ENDERMEN

It is well documented that the enderman will not attack an explorer without provocation. Many builders find a docile enderman rather infuriating, however,

telling tales of their constructions being brought to ruin by the enderman removing and replacing blocks.

Studies have revealed that the enderman will not pick up just any block but will choose only clay, dirt and sand, flowers and other plants, and, rather oddly, TNT. No pattern or purpose has been discerned for this tinkering, although some claim the enderman is indulging us in a form of play, or attempting to communicate.

FACING THE ENDERMAN

But an angry enderman is a very different proposition. Reports from vanquished heroes speak of its strength as an opponent, and it is all too easy to enrage. If it should catch you looking at its body or head it will shake with fury, let out an otherworldly cry, and sprint toward its "aggressor" intent on attack.

Twice the toughness of a zombie, and striking with nearly twice its force, one must be prepared for a fierce battle. But if only this was all. The enderman will usually try to teleport after it is hit, often reappearing in a spot behind its foe. For those who take on the ender dragon, endermen are a particular threat, easy to forget when one's attention is focused on the larger enemy.

Some warriors expose endermen to water by fighting them next to rivers or pouring it from a bucket. Others catch them in spider webs to prevent teleporting, and some fight them from a three-block-high shelter, which they are too tall to enter.

One cannot rely on the following as a distraction, but endermen seem to hate endermites. If an endermite should materialize near an enderman, it will become infuriated, breaking from fighting an adventurer to attack.

Those wishing to avoid the enderman's rage might use a pumpkin head. For reasons science has not yet revealed, adventurers wearing pumpkins on their heads may look at an enderman without incurring its wrath. Could the pumpkin have some special meaning in the End?

Fig. XII.

An early field sketch of an enderman clutching a solid block of clay.

Unsettling eyes glow a sinister shade of violet.

Fig. XIII.

Cross-section of an enderman. Note the large brain.

Purple particles floating around the enderman may be related to their teleportation abilities.

The enderman has unnaturally long legs and arms, particularly compared to its body.

Fig. XIV.

A lone polar bear in a
neutral state.

The stocky polar bear
has ample body mass,
and is well suited to
life in colder biomes.

White fur allows it to
blend into the snowy
landscape and evade
predators.

Pronounced snout
helps the polar bear
sniff out fish.

Strong paws enable the
polar bear to cover ground
quickly and swim through
water with ease.

POLAR BEAR

This dweller of the frozen wastelands is the only mob we currently know to be protective of its young. When angered, the polar bear rears back on its hind legs to strike a splendidly imposing figure. But if one takes care not to anger it, one will find the polar bear of the Overworld is a gentle beast. It is also perfectly adapted to its frozen homelands, which are so devoid of life.

A WINTER NATIVE

I have discovered polar bears across the blasted ice plains, in the crags of the ice mountains and among cruel ice spikes. They have found a niche in these seemingly inhospitable places, their densely furred skin thick with body fat to keep them warm.

They are generally found in pairs of a parent and its cub, leading many researchers to wonder if the natural preference of an adult polar bear is to be alone. They certainly do not tend to congregate, and in their wandering state, adult bears will be neutral to both explorer and mobs alike.

FEARLESS PROTECTOR

Venture near its cub, though, and the adult will be quick to attack. With a roar, it will give chase and bat at its aggressor with its great front claws. Such hostile mobs as zombies and skeletons do not attack bears or earn the adult's anger simply by being in the vicinity, but if they should accidentally hit them, they will suffer the bear's retribution. Bear attacks can often be fatal: they hit with considerable strength and can move with surprising speed, their cubs following close behind in such a fashion that their parents always stand between them and the threat.

Despite the polar bear's reluctance for companionship with its own kind, its parental instinct will extend to other bears' cubs. This devotion to the next generation is not witnessed in any other species, even the rather more social and sophisticated villager.

It is not easy to fight a polar bear. It has been found that if one attempts to aim at its head with sword or arrow, it proves curiously skilled at avoiding damage. One must therefore aim at its hefty body, which is not so easy, since during an attack it will tend to barrel head-first toward its target. Thus, one must press close to its head, and put oneself in danger, so that its body might be reached with one's sword. Avoid confrontation in the first place.

If one should be victorious against a polar bear, it will drop fish, which are its main source of food. They are rather more likely to leave up to two less-appetizing raw fish, but in some cases will drop up to two of the rarer and delicious salmon.

BEAR OF THE WATER

Polar bears are often found near seas, rivers and lakes, since they love the water. You and I may consider the idea of leaping into a near-frozen lake or sea quite horrifying, but the polar bear seems to revel in such activity, even though its shaggy fur takes many hours to fully dry.

Of course, it's just as well that the polar bear enjoys swimming, given the nature and location of its favorite food. Though such behavior has not been witnessed, the polar bear must use its skill in order to catch salmon and other fishy food. Indeed, the bear is a fine swimmer, certainly the best of all land mobs, and can easily outpace any adventurer.

The polar bear's liking for swimming has resulted in a rather clever response in the event that it is set on fire. It will hurry toward the nearest body of water in order to douse the flames.

SPIDER

The monstrously large spiders of the Overworld seem to be particularly complex. They are fickle beasts, neutral toward adventurers at one moment, hostile to them the next. But if one can get into the mind of the spider, it does not need to be an especial threat. Here, we shall do just this. (A brief note: do not confuse the spider with the rather more dangerous cave spider.)

SPIDER HABITAT

The spider is a creature of the dark. It appears in clusters of four in the Overworld at night, in the shadows of forests and in caves. But spiders are not afraid of the light and they will wander in daylight, too.

Spiders are quicker than most mobs, and can jump and climb. They can fit through narrow, one-block spaces. It is therefore common to find oneself coming face-to-face with a spider in surprising circumstances: on roofs, among rafters and other tricky places. And if one should find oneself chased by a spider, it can be a trial to escape. One way of preventing spiders from climbing is to build projections at the top of walls, out from which the spider cannot climb. An overhanging roof, for example, can prevent spiders from getting on top of it, and coming down one's chimney.

ARACHNID BEHAVIOR

But why would a spider attack? Despite much study, I have been unable to draw any definite conclusion. The spider will leave adventurers alone in bright places, and even seem curious and friendly, watching their actions intently. That is, unless it should be harmed by the adventurer, whereupon the spider will attack in retaliation.

During the night or in dark places, however, the spider is aggressive indeed. Its aggression is made more dangerous by the nature of its dark coloring, which can make spiders hard to discern in the gloom. Always watch for their glowing red eyes and listen for their distinctive hiss.

Many scholars have found that an angered spider will continue to attack in bright places, but I have found that there is a way to break its rage: if it should be harmed by something else, like a cactus or fall, it will forget its original target and leave you alone.

Spiders are well worth fighting because they drop two useful items. Most frequently, one will find that they drop string, an important component of bows, leads and fishing rods. Less frequently, one will find they drop a spider eye, which is most useful for brewing potions of poison, or may be fermented to brew various other deadly potions, including harming. It is not known why the spider's eye is so lethal, since the common spider itself does not deliver any poison.

RARE TALENTS

The spider has many remarkable and hair-raising talents, such as an ability to follow the flight of an adventurer's arrow in order to locate them, and it cannot be poisoned with, for example, an arrow of poison.

One should also be aware of the existence of some unusually powerful and rare spiders. The spider jockey is discussed elsewhere, but those adventurers exploring hard worlds will also occasionally come across enchanted versions of these beasts. They are not all alike. Some are fast, some are invisible, some strong and some regenerate their health.

Thankfully the spider is not resilient against a stout sword. Regardless, one must never drop one's guard when faced with this artful arachnid.

Fig. XV.

Dissected view of a common Overworld spider showing silk production system.

The dark gray coloring and larger size helps to distinguish the common spider from its cave-dwelling cousin.

Silk sac is located toward the back of the spider's abdomen.

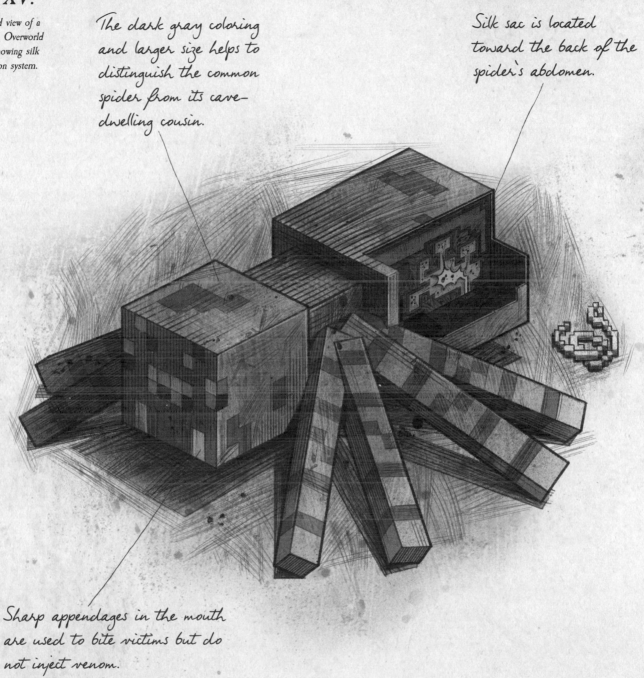

Sharp appendages in the mouth are used to bite victims but do not inject venom.

Fig. XVI.

The dreadful sight of a zombie pigman spotted wandering across the Nether.

The pigman's flesh appears to be afflicted with a wasting disease.

Labored grunting sounds emanate from what is presumably the pigman's mouth.

In several places the skin has completely decomposed and bone is visible.

Garbed in a crude loincloth, the zombie pigman is otherwise unclothed.

ZOMBIE PIGMAN

These damaged creatures can be found wandering in the hellish depths of the Nether. Bearing dirty swords of gold and garbed in tattered clothes, historians have come to the conclusion that zombie pigmen are the remnants of a once-proud race of pigmen which has now, sadly, fallen. No definitive archaeological evidence has yet been discovered of their civilization, however.

HAUNTS OF ZOMBIE PIGMEN

The zombie pigman's rotting flesh falls from its bones, and it emits guttural groans and squeals. Despite this brutish appearance, it is quite peaceful if left alone. But they are quick to anger if they are attacked, a state that one would do best to avoid.

They are most often found slowly traipsing across the vast expanses of netherrack in large groups, occasionally accompanied by their skull-headed babies. But zombie pigmen are not strangers to the Overworld, and many hardy adventurers have recorded them having apparently traveled through Nether portals. There have been very rare accounts of pigs being spontaneously transformed into zombie pigmen by lightning strikes.

ANGERED PIGMEN

To an experienced adventurer, a lone zombie pigman is not a notable threat. They are only as tough as a zombie (but are resistant to fire), and while they can deliver violent blows with their swords they are easily defeated with a sturdy sword and shield.

En masse, however, they pose a much greater threat. When attacked, a pigman will call out to its comrades for aid. Those few who have survived a zombie pigman attack describe facing a wall of decomposing pork, rumbling snorts and slashing swords. By turning and running one might have a chance of survival, but enraged zombie pigmen will pursue their prey over long distances. As they catch sight of their target, they will call out, often attracting more pigmen into the chase.

If you manage to escape, a zombie pigman will calm itself and forget its aggressor after around forty seconds. However, if you should jump into a portal back to the Overworld, they will still be angry on your return. It has been suggested that the Nether is held in suspension while we are in the Overworld. Perhaps the Nether exists on a separate plane of time?

FIGHTING ZOMBIE PIGMEN

Personally, I believe that battling the zombie pigman is worth the considerable risk. Many adventurers report these poor savages drop gold items on death. The most common are gold nuggets, which may be used to prepare golden carrots and glistering melons. In rare cases, if directly killed by an adventurer, pigmen will drop their golden swords and even gold ingots. Callous adventurers avoid awakening the pigmen's rage by killing each one in a single hit, thus preventing individuals from calling out. It is hard to condone such brutality, but they say it can be achieved by swigging a potion of strength II, taking a diamond axe in hand, and jumping down on one's target to perform what they rather tastelessly call "a critical hit."

One might justify such violence when one considers the zombie pigman's hatred for the villagers. They will mercilessly hunt these innocent homesteaders, killing them in their homes. What bygone events could have incited this barbarousness?

Some explorers have reported that on October 31, zombie pigmen celebrate a strange festival, carrying pumpkins and wearing them on their heads.

UTILITY MOBS

◆

It is possible to craft two mobs which will be naturally
inclined to protect their creator from hostile mob attacks.
Let us look at how to bring these utility mobs to life,
and how they may be of use.

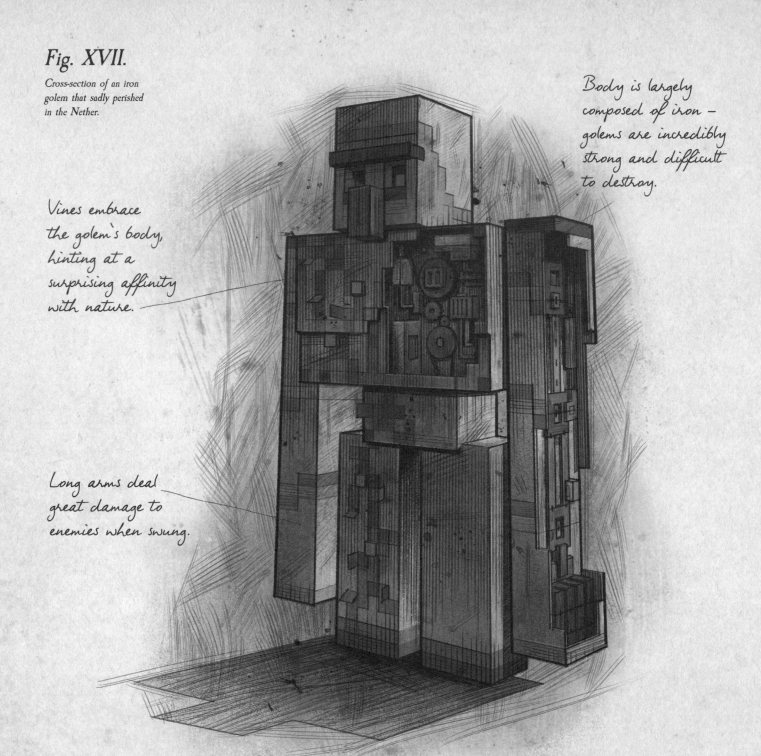

Fig. XVII.

Cross-section of an iron golem that sadly perished in the Nether.

Body is largely composed of iron — golems are incredibly strong and difficult to destroy.

Vines embrace the golem's body, hinting at a surprising affinity with nature.

Long arms deal great damage to enemies when swung.

IRON GOLEM

Not all inhabitants of this world wish harm to adventurers. Indeed, some will lend their fabulous strength and resilience, the mightiest being the iron golems. These giants are capable of great brutality and can withstand vast amounts of damage. Only the wither and ender dragon can endure more. It is most fortunate, therefore, that the iron golems are on our side.

THE VILLAGE GOLEMS

Though iron golems are customarily made by their masters, wanderers of the Overworld will naturally come across them guarding villages with ten or more villagers living in them. It is not exactly understood how villagers summon their iron golems, but sooner or later, one is sure to appear.

Villagers seem to have a very close relationship with their vine-strewn guardians, and appear to communicate with them. (Despite many attempts, I have never successfully managed to exchange words with an iron golem.) Iron golems are also known to pick up poppies and hold them in their hand for the delight of their villager friends. Child villagers have been witnessed approaching the golem and taking the flower from them. This is surely one of the worlds' most delightful sights.

GOLEMS IN BATTLE

Iron golems patrol the village to which they belong and attack anything which hurts a villager. Since villagers are most commonly targeted by zombies, those shambling brutes are the iron golem's commonest foe, and they have mastered the art of killing them with just one or two swings of their arms. The strength of an iron golem's blow can vary considerably, but at its most powerful, the only thing more damaging is a creeper's explosion and the golem's target is often sent flying. Golems' long arms can also reach right through a single-block wall.

Iron golems will never be hurt by any fall, and they do not drown. And yet they are not invincible. Beware, in particular, of zombie hordes. In the sad event of their death, iron golems drop between three and five iron ingots and up to two poppies.

A heartless adventurer who considers attacking a villager would do well to note the formidable powers of the iron golem. A village's golem will attack anyone who threatens its friends. And for those thinking that the looting enchantment might make iron golems a fine source of iron, they are somehow able to resist this enchantment. For most warriors, battling an iron golem is not worth the risk.

SUMMONING A GOLEM

Constructing one's own golem is a practical way to defend one's homestead. It will defend any nearby villager and remain loyal to its creator. But it will not follow its creator unless attached by a lead.

Given the powers of the iron golem, one may be surprised by the simplicity of its construction, which merely requires four iron blocks and a pumpkin. Iron blocks are crafted from nine iron ingots, thus 36 iron ore is required in total. The iron blocks are arranged in a T-shape, and a pumpkin is placed on the top. Once complete, the iron golem is immediately animated into life.

The pumpkin must always be placed last, and there must be nothing occupying the spaces below the figure's arms. These appear to interfere with the energies that give the iron golem life. The configuration does not need to be vertical, however. Through experimentation I have discovered that it may be constructed as if lying down, and even upside-down.

SNOW GOLEM

There is but one known mob which is only brought into existence if created by an adventurer. The snow golem, a strange, wintry fellow, shares much with the iron golem, but lacks its strength and resilience. A snow golem has several uses which may make an explorer's life better, despite the rather frightful appearance of its head. It is merely a helmet, however.

CONSTRUCTION

A snow golem is constructed in a similar manner to the iron golem. Two snow blocks are set, one on top of the other, and then a pumpkin or jack-o'-lantern is placed on top. (The same configuration also works on its side, or upside down.) This rite of substantiation immediately infuses the snow golem with life.

A brief clarification: it has come to my attention that snow golems may appear without being created by an adventurer. The enderman's tendency to pick up blocks may lead it to pick up a pumpkin, and then it may, by coincidence, happen to place it on a stack of snow blocks. The likelihood of this is, of course, rather low, but reports of it have been heard.

The snow golem shares the coal buttons and stick arms of a happy children's snowman, but its pumpkin head glowers rather dreadfully. We are sure, however, that it is no threat to us. If one should decide to get rid of a snow golem, it will fall to a single sweep of an adventurer's wooden sword, and it melts after just seconds in the hot climates of deserts, jungles, savanna, mesas, and the Nether.

USES OF SNOW GOLEMS

A snow golem does not interact with its maker, and will not follow them unless pulled by a lead. It moves by placing a thin layer of snow below its lower body, and then slides across it.

In cooler climates, such as taiga, extreme hills, but also plains and forest and the End, the golem will leave this layer of snow behind it. This is one of the benefits of the snow golem, for it offers a fantastic supply of snowballs or snow blocks for those attempting to build an igloo. One may quickly collect large quantities by trapping a snow golem in a single-block space with its lower half exposed. The golem will rapidly secrete snow, and does not appear to mind at all.

SNOWBALL WARRIOR

A snow golem's most obvious use is as a guard, but it is rather less effective than an iron golem. Its only weapon is the snowball, which it throws at a rate of about one a second at any hostile beast it encounters. These snowballs do their targets no damage, and merely serve to knock them backward a little way. But when threats are pressing, sometimes having them knocked back can make all the difference. Remember, however, that one's snow golem must be protected, since it can only withstand a single zombie bite.

Explorers of the Nether will be pleased to hear of the snowball's effectiveness against the blaze, but the snow golem melts in the Nether's heat. One can protect one's golems with splash potions of fire resistance, but most warriors prefer to arm themselves with snowballs.

While the golem will do no damage against the enderman, each snowball that hits its target will cause the enderman to teleport, affording one some protection through distraction. And some warriors like to build a gang of golems on their visits to the End, where angering endermen is a continual danger.

Fig. XVIII.

Recent sketch of a snow golem shortly after I created it.

The body is formed of two blocks of snow and is fairly weak.

In all but the hottest biomes, the golem will leave a trail of snow in its wake.

The golem's stick arms appear to be largely useless.

Buttons, apparently made of coal, decorate the golem's body.

HOSTILE MOBS

Now we come to the horrors of this strange world – the hostile mobs. These creatures are full of malice and are intent on your destruction. Much concentration is required when studying the following pages.

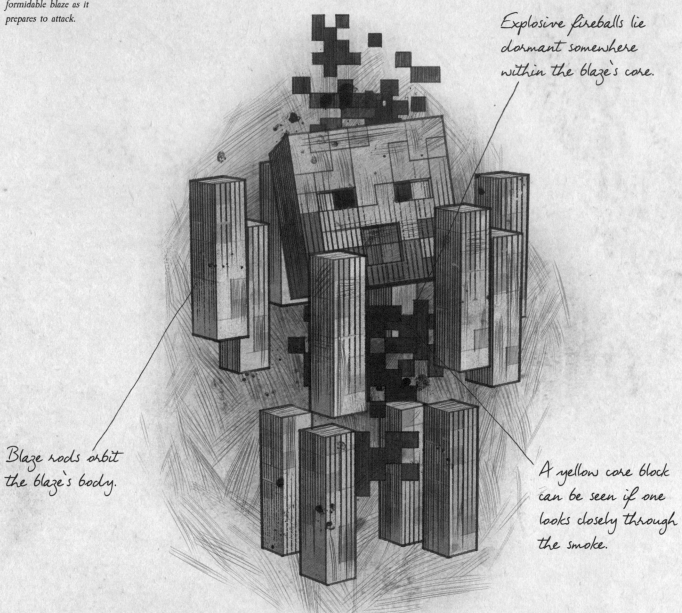

Explosive fireballs lie dormant somewhere within the blaze's core.

Blaze rods orbit the blaze's body.

A yellow core block can be seen if one looks closely through the smoke.

BLAZE

The first account of the fearsome blaze was provided by one of the pioneers of the Nether. Scrawled on a scrap of paper, it described a creature made of fire, preventing exploration of a Nether fortress. The note was found sometime later, and there was no sign of the explorer. It is no surprise, since blazes throw explosive fireballs at anyone who should come close.

BLAZE PHYSIOLOGY

We know today that the blaze is not made from fire. When one spies a specimen in an idle state, one will see that its body is actually a yellow block with several rods circling it. In this idle state, the blaze will not generally fly, preferring to bob across the ground instead, or to swim in lava. Explorers of the Nether are advised to listen out for its distinctive groaning roar, for when a blaze sees an explorer, it will envelop its body in flames and rise up, ready for conflict.

The blaze does not spontaneously exist in the Nether; rather, it is conjured into existence by a spawner, seemingly programmed to protect Nether fortresses from any intruder.

FIGHTING FIRE

The blaze fights from a distance, bombarding its foes with volleys of three fireballs. Each shot strikes with much force and will set its target ablaze, but if one should think that its inaccuracy is its weakness, consider that when fighting on flammable netherrack, fireballs which miss will set the ground around one into scorching chaos. It is recommended that one take a potion of fire resistance in preparation, which protects against blazes' blasts and the fires they cause.

I have found that the best weapon to use against the blaze is the snowball, which will defeat a blaze in seven strikes. The snowball's ranged nature also avoids the blaze's strong melee attack, against which fire resistance is useless. As such, it is highly recommended that any Nether trip is preceded by a visit to a snowy biome or mountaintop to collect snowballs, or to harvest the stuff from one's own snow golem. Explorers are also advised to carry a water bucket, for putting out fires as well as for pouring onto a blaze. This technique is not easy to achieve, but is most effective.

An alternative strategy is to use the blaze's rather foolish tendency to attack anything that harms it, including other blazes. By positioning oneself between angry blazes, one might induce a battle between them. Whichever method one uses, remember to focus attention on the blazes' spawner as soon as possible to prevent more from arriving. Unless, of course, one is harvesting the rather useful items that they drop.

THE SPOILS OF BLAZES

Blazes are terrible beasts, but they are the source of a fabulously useful item which leads many adventurers to hunt them – the blaze rod. It is hot and smells of sulphur, and studies have shown that it stores a great deal of energy. The blaze uses this energy to generate the fires around it and the hot gases that allow it to fly, and also to produce its fireballs.

Unfortunately, science has not yet unlocked access to this boundless energy, but blaze rods may be crafted with cobblestone to provide the heat source for brewing stands. Even more importantly, it also produces blaze powder, which fuels the brewing stand and creates several highly useful items, including eyes of ender, which are used to open a portal to the End. Any explorer wishing to reach the End, then, will need to defeat many blazes. I wish them great luck.

CHICKEN JOCKEY

The chicken jockey makes us question all we know about the natural order of things. What could possibly induce a chicken into allowing a rotting baby zombie to sit astride its back? And what guides the baby zombie's bizarre compulsion to mount a chicken? This ridiculous pairing really makes one's stomach turn.

CHICKEN JOCKEY HABITATS

If there is a single fact about this union between chicken and zombie that illustrates its sheer unnaturalness, it is this: if one was to fling a splash potion of healing at a chicken jockey, it will harm the zombie because it is undead, and heal the chicken. If one were to fling a potion of harming at it, the chicken will be harmed because it is alive, and the zombie will be healed.

Thankfully, the chicken jockey is a very rare occurrence. While this pairing occurs most frequently in the chicken's natural grassy habitats in the Overworld, it can also appear where no chicken is usually found. They may even be witnessed wandering the Nether, where, instead of a baby zombie, the chicken is ridden by a baby zombie pigman. Interestingly, zombie pigman jockeys act just as zombie pigmen do, which is to say that they will only attack an adventurer if they are provoked.

It is estimated that one is likely to encounter one chicken jockey for every 200 zombies in those areas where chickens live, and one for every 400 in areas where chickens do not live. And besides common zombies and zombie pigmen, baby zombie villagers may also be seen as the rider.

BEHAVIOR AND HABITS

The chicken appears to be closely controlled by the zombie, and therefore moves about much like a baby zombie, far faster than a chicken's natural walking speed. If the pair should fall from a height, the chicken's wings will bring them down safely, so we can assume that some of its sense of self-preservation remains. Moreover, a chicken jockey which is not intent on attacking may be led with seeds. This is most commonly achieved on chickens ridden by peaceful zombie pigmen. It seems that the rider does not have complete control over its steed. Notably, however, the chicken seems unable to lay eggs. This may be an indication of the stress the poor creature is under.

Although the chicken jockey acts as one, it is not a single unit. The chicken or the zombie may be killed, leaving the other alive. Thus, if a warrior strikes the chicken down, its rider will be able to continue the attack. It is a challenge not to hit the rider: one must generally aim one's strikes directly at the chicken's feet to be successful. If the rider is killed, the chicken will thankfully not continue the attack and can thus be allowed to go free. Both the chicken and its rider will drop their customary items when they are killed.

POINTS OF INTEREST

More evidence of the tensions between the rider and its steed are to be seen in the rare case of a chicken jockey entering a single block-high space. Several journals describe the chicken being able to run quite freely, and yet the zombie suffocates in the block above. In cases where the zombie died, the chicken contentedly trotted onward, as if nothing had happened. Quite inexplicable.

The chicken is not the only creature that is ridden by the undead. Readers will find entries on the skeletal horseman and spider jockey in later pages of this book. They are also terrible pairings.

Fig. XX.

The dreadful chicken jockey (zombie variant).

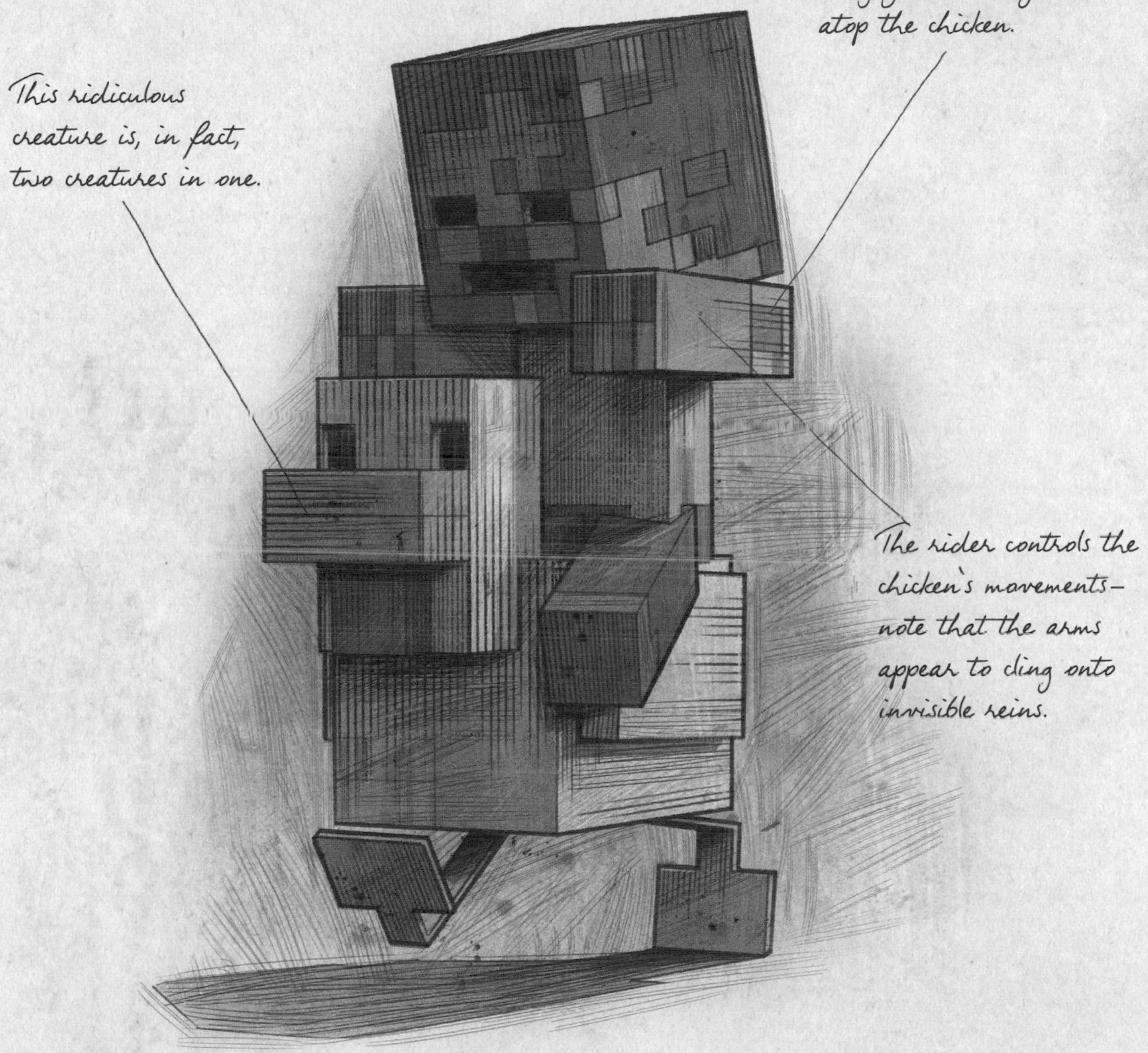

This ridiculous creature is, in fact, two creatures in one.

A baby zombie, a baby zombie pigman or a baby zombie villager sits atop the chicken.

The rider controls the chicken's movements— note that the arms appear to cling onto invisible reins.

Fig. XXI.

A stalking creeper sketched during one of my early adventures.

Tiny brain is programmed to stalk adventurers and to detonate the TNT when it can do maximum devastation.

The creeper's permanently downturned mouth suggests a profound sadness.

Fig. XXII.

This cross-section diagram is based on the body parts found after a creeper attempted to detonate when partly submerged in water.

The center of gravity is low. Its four short legs enable it to scuttle about in almost complete silence.

CREEPER

It is hard to understand the modern appeal of memorabilia depicting this monster, and yet the ancient desert temples clearly portray its image too. What is behind this perplexing popularity? Perhaps it is because they are so common, or is it their contradictory nature? Every adventurer has met one of these frightening beasts, yet it is also somewhat ridiculous in appearance.

CREEPER HABITATS

Creepers are found everywhere in the Overworld where darkness can be found, in caverns, in deep forests, and at night. But they do not burn in sunlight. It is easy to be taken by surprise by a creeper, since the first you will hear of its presence is the awful hiss of it priming itself to explode. Etymologists suggest the creeper was named after this silent stalking.

A creeper explosion will instantly kill any adventurer standing next to it, even if they are wearing full diamond armor, and seriously injure those within three or four blocks. But many adventurers fear the creeper for its capacity to destroy their constructions.

EXPLOSIVE POWER

The evidence, gathered at great risk, indicates that the explosion is caused by the build-up of high-pressure gas within the creeper's body, causing a blast only slightly less powerful than exploding TNT. But why does the creeper destroy itself in the process? Some say that the explosions distribute spores from which new creepers grow.

Others argue that creepers simply wish to cause us ill. It is difficult to know for certain.

The creeper begins an unfairly short second-and-a-half countdown when a block away from an adventurer. To prevent detonation, the adventurer must immediately put some distance between themselves and the creeper. Four blocks will suffice, but sometimes less will be enough. If a creeper's countdown is cut short, it cannot prime itself again for a short period, so you will be temporarily safe.

Be aware, too, of the charged creeper, distinct for its glowing green aura. These are created if lightning should strike nearby, and cause an explosion of twice a creeper's normal power. Trophy hunters prize them: if a charged creeper kills zombies, skeletons, wither skeletons or creepers, they will drop their mob heads.

FIGHTING THE CREEPER

I find the bow is the best weapon to use against a creeper, since fighting them at close-quarters is perilous. If one has no choice, consider adding the knockback enchantment to your sword, although sprint-hits achieve a similar effect. You may be able to catch creepers in cobwebs, in which they cannot explode. And always run backward to escape, as it is unlikely one will have time to turn first. Creeper battles are worthwhile, since the creeper drops gunpowder, which can be crafted into TNT, splash potions and fireworks.

There is no perfect way to protect a home against the creeper, other than to build it from blast-resistant obsidian. Clearly this is not practical. Thus, the best strategies are to light areas well to prevent creepers appearing nearby. Build trenches to catch them (a creeper cannot jump more than a block in height). A creeper's explosive blast damage will be significantly reduced in water, so a moat can help. Creepers are afraid of ocelots and cats, so having some roaming about one's home can help. Most of all, exercise vigilance. It is the best defense against hearing the click-hiss that can be one's doom.

ELDER GUARDIAN

Scholars were taken aback when explorers discovered large temples deep beneath the sea and the beasts that haunt them. We know the guardians cannot have built ocean temples themselves. But they protect them, and the grotesque elder guardian is their master. A fearsome creature, the elder guardian is the reason my studies of ocean temples are incomplete.

ELDER GUARDIAN HABITAT

Three elder guardians will be found within the chambers of ocean monuments. They can easily be identified from lesser guardians since they are twice as large and deathly pale. Their skin is cracked, as if carved from some ancient rock, and their single white eye stares with a gaze that is somehow both unknowable and cruel. Thankfully, they move less energetically than guardians.

The elder guardian's connection to ocean temples means it is rare, and it seems to be becoming rarer, since it has no means of reproducing. As brave adventurers slay them, elders never seem to return. (The scientific community has considered sending out parties to eradicate them once and for all, but new ocean temples are discovered daily, and the damage to our fighters would be heavy indeed.)

BATTLING THE HORROR

The elder guardian shares many of its offensive abilities with the guardian, and so for wider discussion of its basic attacks, please consult that entry. But the elder has some unique capabilities. Most evident is its toughness. Capable of taking nearly three times the damage of a guardian, the elder is a force to be reckoned with. Its own attacks – both by laser beam and body spikes – are more deadly, too.

Should an explorer manage to vanquish an elder guardian, it will drop up to two prismarine shards, a substance which when crafted together makes prismarine blocks of various types, the very substance from which ocean temples are made. It can also often drop a prismarine crystal, which can create sea lanterns.

Elder guardians will also drop a water-absorbing sponge if killed by an adventurer, and if it doesn't drop a prismarine crystal, one will find raw fish of some kind in its place. Some scholars think that this is evidence that its diet consists of fish and other natural watery foodstuff, but guardians have never been seen to wander far from their temple homes to catch them, and so we cannot be sure. Elder guardians and guardians may also be seen to ferociously attack any squid that ventures close. We do not know why – a squid surely presents little threat to an ocean temple, or, indeed, to the well-being of their fearsome inhabitants.

PROTECTOR OF TEMPLES

The elder guardian is capable of detecting adventurers from great distances. Any adventurer within 50 blocks will experience a terrifying attack in which the elder guardian's ghostly form appears before them and swoops around their body. The unlucky victim is not caused any actual harm, but is cursed with an affliction that causes a strong form of mining fatigue which lasts five minutes and slows mining by many factors. (It is advised that one drinks milk to counteract this sickness.)

Most scholars believe that the elder guardian is some kind of protector of the temple: by preventing intruders from mining, they cannot damage it. We do not understand why the temple is so important to the elder guardian. If they cannot breed, they may be as old as the stones themselves.

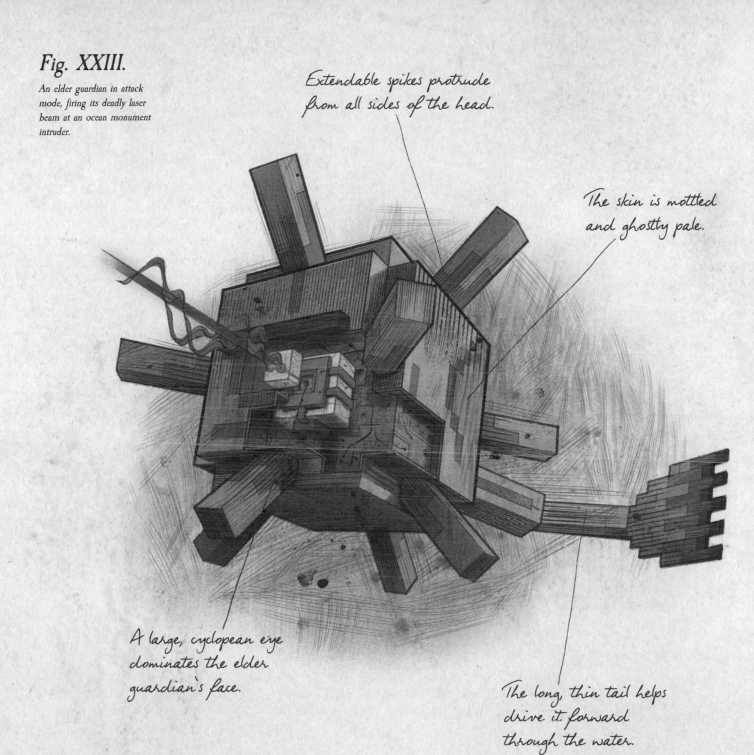

Fig. XXIII.

An elder guardian in attack mode, firing its deadly laser beam at an ocean monument intruder.

Extendable spikes protrude from all sides of the head.

The skin is mottled and ghostly pale.

A large, cyclopean eye dominates the elder guardian's face.

The long, thin tail helps drive it forward through the water.

Fig. XXIV.

Field sketch of a small
group of endermites.

A trail of purple
particles can be detected
behind the endermite.

Note the simple anatomy:
a small, stunted head juts
out from a cuboid body.

The single eye betrays
no thought but malice.

ENDERMITE

Much is peculiar about the End. Questions about where it could be situated still perplex scientists. And then there is the endermite. How could the smallest mob yet encountered pose one of the biggest questions? The endermite is a pest, a biting nuisance of such small size that it is hard to hit with one's sword. It is certainly a repellent creature.

HOW ENDERMITES APPEAR

The endermite may only be discovered as a result of teleportation with the use of an ender pearl. The ender pearl is an item dropped by endermen that, when thrown, causes its thrower to jump immediately to the location where it falls. Occasionally an endermite will appear at one's feet and promptly begin a ferocious attack.

As a result of some uncomfortable experimentation (each individual act of teleportation causes small injury), I have come to the conclusion that an endermite will appear at a rate of about one in every twenty jumps.

FIGHTING ENDERMITES

Endermites do not bite with much strength, but are highly determined and much tougher than they appear to be. Indeed, they are able to take two standard blows from even a diamond sword. Some adventurers like to employ the bane of arthropods enchantment so that they might kill them in a single strike. But such effort is ultimately futile, as there is no apparent reward for finishing them off.

Historical records indicate that there was a time when the endermen's teleportation would also generate endermites. Happily, this is no longer the case, which must be of some comfort to these creatures (if they experience such feelings), since the enderman detests the endermite. It is amusing to think that something so small should cause an enderman such annoyance, but adventurers have described battling endermen only to see them going off after the pests and forgetting about them entirely.

ORIGINS OF ENDERMITES

One might assume that endermites live in the End, given their name. But they have not been found there, except as a consequence of ender pearl jumps. This leads many researchers to believe that they live in a place between dimensions.

Other scholars have suggested that endermites' trails of purple particles resemble those of endermen. But with closer examination one will see that they behave differently. The particles seem to be attracted to one another, causing them to converge and then pop out of existence. Fascinatingly, the endermite also has the ability to pop out of existence itself. The forces (or is it magic?) which cause the appearance of endermites will apparently cause them to disappear after exactly two minutes of existence, regardless of whether they are in view of an adventurer or not.

So what is an endermite? Some argue it is a trans-dimensional parasite that pulls itself along with anything traveling between worlds, before it is reclaimed by the void from which it came. This may explain why endermen, who freely travel between the End and Overworld, hate them.

But I have to wonder whether its vulnerability to the bane of arthropods may indicate that the endermite is related to the Overworld's spiders and silverfish. Perhaps both theories are correct, and the endermite is evidence that beings have traveled to the Overworld for millennia? Oh, all these questions are quite enough to give one a headache.

EVOKER

Deep within the thickest forests, one might stumble upon a building that will strike fear into the bravest heart. These large mansions sit in the gloom and two sinister creatures occupy them. Known as illagers, they are outcasts from the friendly villages we know and love, twisted by their practice of evil. The evoker is one of these, a practicer of foul magics and trickery.

THE DARK SORCERER

Chillingly, evokers stand like any villager, wearing black robes with a golden trim. But their gray skin betrays their true identity. Warped by hatred, they will attack any explorer, villager or iron golem on sight. In fact, though they do not exhibit malice toward them, they appear to shun their own kind, too, since they are always found alone and only in certain rooms in the mansion.

A world will only have a certain number of evokers resident within it. Their evil is thus contained, since no new evokers will ever be able to spawn, but this also means that once discovered, an evoker will remain present at its location until an adventurer is able to vanquish it.

INTO THE JAWS OF DEATH

Evokers' attacks are strange indeed. The first is the conjuration of a series of ghostly fangs, which rise from the ground in a wave and give a single vicious snap to the legs of any adventurer or mob standing in their way, before they sink back again.

So sharp are their bites that they cut straight through any armor, and even through any enchantments.

The evoker deploys its fangs in two different patterns. If it is three or more blocks away from its target, it will send 16 fangs in a line toward its prey. If its prey is closer, 13 fangs appear in a ring around the evoker, hitting anything within its circumference. It is recommended that one either keeps it at range or lunges at it with a quick melee strike before retreating, since its defensive attack is difficult to avoid.

One might also attempt to engage an evoker with a block nearby for cover, since its fangs cannot penetrate nor rise over walls if you remain low behind them. The creature will announce its intention to use its fangs with a low chiming sound and purple smoke issuing from its outstretched arms.

VEXATIOUS SUMMONING

The evoker's second attack is to summon a strange and malevolent imp, the vex. Discussion of this flying menace can be found later in this book, but its summoning is signaled by another, higher, horn sound and a puff of white smoke. The vexes will appear in groups of between two and four for each summoning, and greatly distract any adventurer in battle with the evoker, leaving them prone to being assaulted by its fangs. If one fails to defeat vexes before the evoker begins to summon more, one runs the risk of being overwhelmed.

Engaging the evoker is perilous, but should one manage to defeat it, the rewards are excellent. The mansion becomes safer to explore, enabling one to discover its mysteries in peace. The evoker may drop an emerald, and will always drop a totem of undying. This strange object has a mystical property which can save an adventurer from a fatal blow. The totem will be destroyed, but its wielder will be left with half a heart of health and will be enchanted with regeneration and absorption. A valuable item indeed.

Evokers appear to hate blue sheep, employing their magic to turn them red. We have no understanding why.

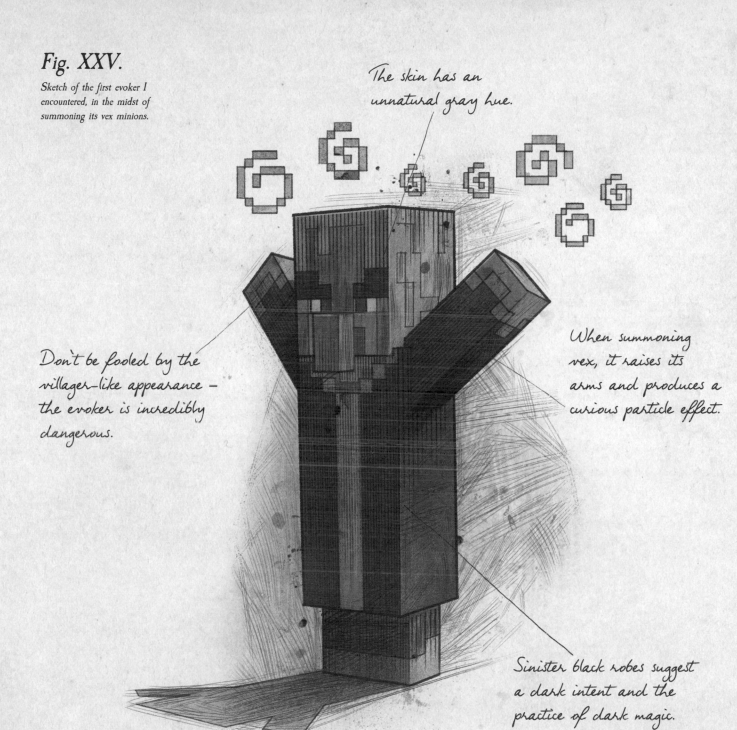

Fig. XXV.

Sketch of the first evoker I encountered, in the midst of summoning its vex minions.

The skin has an unnatural gray hue.

Don't be fooled by the villager-like appearance — the evoker is incredibly dangerous.

When summoning vex, it raises its arms and produces a curious particle effect.

Sinister black robes suggest a dark intent and the practice of dark magic.

Fig. XXVI.

Field sketch of a ghast in attack mode as it releases a fireball.

Immense body is four blocks wide and deep and covered with scars.

The tracks of tears once shed are visible on the ghast's face.

Stomach is largely filled with fireballs.

GHAST

easuring four blocks deep, four blocks high and four blocks wide, and with grotesque feelers dangling below it, to know the Nether-dwelling ghast is to truly know horror. Its face wears a sad expression and its cry is mournful, but as soon as it releases a volley of scorching fireballs in your direction, it becomes clear that this is part of a dreadful trick.

FIREBALLS AND SHELTER

Many adventurers have recorded accounts of their meetings with these terrible beasts, and comparison of their experiences has revealed that ghasts spawn in any room-sized space in the Nether. For some adventurers, this has even been known to occur within the confines of their shelters, and so it is advised that any Nether encampment be kept as small as possible. The ghast is highly dangerous at range, too, having remarkable perception which enables it to spy its prey across distances as great as a hundred blocks.

The ghast has just one attack, but it is violent. Its explosive fireballs are powerful enough to burst through netherrack, and can cause extremely serious injury, first with their impact, and then with their explosive effect.

Fortunately, cobblestone is durable enough to withstand these explosions. One can therefore use it to build cover; some explorers have constructed entire tunnel systems in order to avoid ghasts' attention. Naturally, this involves bringing stone to the Nether, but if one's supply should dwindle, one can cook netherrack in a furnace to make the more durable Nether brick. Many other blocks have been found to be suitable, too, including stone, granite and iron.

CONQUERING THE GHAST

Fortunately, the ghast has a weakness. Its soft body is almost entirely filled with gas, and may easily be punctured. Consequently, some ghasts have been defeated with no more than a stone pickaxe. Their tendency to float out of reach makes attacking them difficult, but sharp-shooting adventurers will find that a pair of carefully aimed arrows will defeat them. In the face of an oncoming fireball, the greatest warriors have been known to bravely stand their ground and strike the fireball just as it is about to hit, sending the flaming orb back from whence it came. A taste of its own medicine indeed.

If a ghast comes near your Nether portal, one must avoid engaging it. A single fireball can obliterate the portal's purple field, and adventurers may find themselves stranded in the Nether. If such a calamity should occur and one does not have a flint and steel, do not panic. I have learned that if one can cause another fireball to strike the inside of the portal's obsidian frame, it will reignite the gateway.

SPOILS OF THE GHAST

Ghasts drop up to two gunpowder, and if one is lucky, the highly prized ghast tear. This item is combined with awkward potions to brew potions of regeneration. But a second use of ghast tears has recently been discovered. With glass and an eye of ender, it constructs the fabulous End crystal, which has the power to revive the ender dragon.

Obtaining these items is a challenge, however. Ghasts are frequently killed over lava, into which the items will fall. Battles at close range are difficult to stage, but with care and patience they might be led by alternately revealing oneself and retreating behind cover. Or one can try something that sounds foolish indeed: some warriors suggest snaring and reeling in ghasts with, of all things, a fishing rod.

GUARDIAN

Like the elder guardian, the guardian patrols the ancient ocean monuments and its awful body is bulbous and spiked with a single, staring eye. But the guardian is half the elder's size and is a shade of turquoise. The scientific community frequently debates whether guardians are a younger form of elder guardian, but the current thinking is that they are a separate species.

FACING THE BEAM

The guardian is remarkably tough, and its attacks are strong. We shall now study the guardian's strengths, and suggest some ways in which adventurers may face them and survive as they attempt to enter ocean monuments.

The first guardian attack that most will encounter is its laser beam. If it can see an adventurer, whether under or above water, it will fix a steady beam of purplish light upon them from its eye, which follows them as they move. The beam is hot, boiling the water around it, though not hot enough to hurt in my experience. But, as it charges, the light changes to yellow, and after three seconds it reaches critical power. Its target will be hit with a bolt of power which delivers about twice as much damage as that of a zombie's attack.

This blast will also penetrate armor, so few are safe. The guardians' large eyes are sensitive enough to detect adventurers at great range in the dark of the sea. But their reliance on sight is their greatest weakness. By hiding behind cover, the guardian will terminate its beam. In fact, those who have faced them will tell you that, unlike many mobs, guardians will seem to forget if they lose sight of their target, and will return to patrolling rather than giving chase. So when approaching guardians, it is advisable to stay close to the ocean floor, use natural cover or have blocks ready to place to build hasty cover.

SPIKE ATTACK

Many inexperienced adventurers think that once they have closed the distance between themselves and a guardian, the battle is won. They are very much mistaken. The guardian is covered in spikes which it can extend and retract at will and they will inflict damage on whoever should attack it. And if one should corner a guardian, it is doubly dangerous. While it prefers not to use its beam at close range, when confined it will try to fire it and use its spikes at the same time.

And yet, one cannot attack a guardian at range, for one cannot effectively shoot arrows under water. It is strongly recommended that one employs the strongest armor, preferably enchanted, for it is almost impossible to avoid damage entirely, even for the greatest of warriors.

NOTES OF INTEREST

Curiously, a guardian will not die when removed from water. It cannot control its movements on land, but it is still dangerous, flapping madly and extending and retracting its spikes. One should keep one's distance, and consider using a bow and arrows to finish it off for good.

If one should successfully kill one of these beasts, one can expect it to drop very much the same items as those dropped by an elder (consultation of its entry will provide details). As for its corpse, a single specimen has been recovered for science. Its eye was badly damaged, so we learned nothing of how it generates its beam, but we did discover that guardians are hollow, with no internal organs. The interior walls of their bodies are red, and their spikes pierce right through them. A most bizarre animal. Fitting, perhaps, given the bizarre places in which it dwells.

Fig. XXVII.

A patrolling guardian sighted just above an ocean temple in a deep ocean biome.

Turquoise skin is identical to the prismarine with which ocean monuments are constructed.

The guardian's eye emits a powerful laser.

Vibrant orange spikes protrude from the body, making close encounters hazardous.

No obvious mouth, but the guardian may drop a fish, so it is likely to be a carnivore.

Fig. XXVIII.

A large magma cube in its resting state and its companion which has elongated to reveal its molten core.

When jumping, the creature's many thin segments separate like the coils of a spring and propel it to remarkable heights.

The large magma cube is the same height as an adventurer.

The eyes are composed of lava and appear to be part of the core.

MAGMA CUBE

I t seems many Nether mobs have become partly flame themselves. One of the clearest examples of this theory is the magma cube. It is surely a cousin to the Overworld's slime and shares many of its behaviors, though the magma cube is made from molten rock and is more dangerous. Explorers should take great care when facing it, and apply the education I shall set forth here.

NATURAL HABITAT

Magma cubes live throughout the Nether, but I have found that their population is particularly dense inside Nether fortresses. Like the slime, it is found in three different sizes, the smallest being the weakest and only a quarter the height of a person, while the largest is about a person's full height.

The magma cube jumps in a similar fashion to the slime, too, but the large magma cube can reach a remarkable four blocks in height. It seems to achieve this feat by separating its thick stony crust in sections, allowing its form to elongate. As it does so, the magma cube's molten core can clearly be seen. As it lands, its weight contracts its stony crust, forcing embers through its cracks which flicker about the ground around it. Jumping appears to cause the magma cube great effort; they are less active than slimes, and are seen leaping around only half as often.

Further proof of how well-adapted a magma cube is to its Nether home is in its ability to withstand lava, through which it moves without taking any damage. It can also withstand falling from the Nether's many towering outcrops, apparently protected by its stony outer layer.

FIGHTING MAGMA CUBES

If a magma cube should spy an explorer, it will clumsily bounce toward them, and attempt to land on top of its victim. Any kind of contact with its hot crust will hurt, dealing damage at twice the rate of most other mobs. As such, one must attempt to gain distance, but the irregularity of timing and distance with which a magma cube can leap makes avoiding injury greatly challenging, even to experienced warriors.

From what we can gather, slimes and magma cubes have identical health, but the thick crust of magma cubes provides them with natural armor which diminishes the power of a warrior's blows. The biggest magma cubes have the most health and the thickest armored crust, making them a formidable opponent for any who should face them without a strong sword – or better, a bow, so they might be fought from a safer distance.

Engaging large or medium-sized magma cubes is not often advised, since when they are killed they will divide into between one and four smaller-sized specimens. Thus, a warrior attempting to defeat a single large cube could ultimately have to fight twenty-one cubes of varying sizes in total.

DROPS OF THE MAGMA CUBE

The items which drop from a magma cube do not give one enormous incentive to battle them, but they inspire much scientific interest. The medium and large-sized specimens occasionally drop a single magma cream, a substance that may be brewed with an awkward potion into a potion of fire resistance, which is useful for exploration of the Nether.

Magma cream may also be created by crafting together blaze powder and a slimeball. Scholars around the Overworld feel this provides evidence of the magma cube's relationship with not only the slime, but also with the blaze. Perhaps its fiery abilities are inherited from that floating terror? Quite fascinating.

SHULKER

We do not know who built the End cities. The buildings are deserted, and the treasures hidden inside are ripe for the taking. Deserted except for shulkers, that is. These creatures sit in wait for intruders, and shoot them with magic missiles. Were they placed there to defend the cities? Are they evidence that the cities' builders plan to return someday?

SHULKER BIOLOGY

These devious creatures clasp their camouflaged shells tightly to walls and floors. Their purple exterior matches that of the purpur blocks from which End cities are constructed. This may be a natural adaptation of the shulker to help conceal it, or it may be engineered by the cities' architects. Discovering which it is will help us better understand this mysterious organism.

The shulker resembles such common crustaceans as limpets, securely attaching itself to horizontal and vertical surfaces by suction with its strong foot. It will periodically open its hard shell, peering out to sense anything which may have strayed into its territory. Researchers such as I who have visited End cities have cracked this hard exterior open to reveal a soft body inside, equipped with two eyes to detect threats, as well as the ability to generate its missiles.

THE MAGIC MISSILE

Fired with a rapid twist of its upper shell, the shulker's enchanted missile is not a fast-moving projectile, but it is dangerous. It seeks its targets, following them until it makes contact. It immediately deals a good amount of injury, and bestows the levitation effect on its target, causing them to be lifted into the air for ten seconds.

If one has a bucket of milk, it would be wise to immediately drink it to remove the levitation effect. This must be done as soon as possible, however, since when the levitation's grip is ended, one will plummet to the ground. Thus the shulker's missile has potential to injure twice over: by hitting the target and then by causing it to fall. And all the time one remains in the air, one is likely to still be within range of the shulker, which will continue to send more missiles toward its target. Many adventurers have fallen, quite literally, after a continued assault from which they could not escape.

DISPOSING OF SHULKERS

One must take great precaution to avoid being hit by a shulker missile. Two methods prove useful. The first is to hit the missile from the air with a carefully timed sword-strike. The second is to run from the missile in such a way that it harmlessly impacts upon the ground or the wall of a nearby building.

It is difficult to attack the shulker itself. When its shell is closed, it is strongly armored. Striking it will only cause a tiny amount of damage, and arrows will be deflected. One must wait for the shell to open, exposing its soft body, but even then, the shulker will need five hits from a standard diamond sword before it perishes. Some warriors employ potions of harming, which have the capacity to penetrate its shell.

Once a shulker is attacked, however, it somehow signals all nearby shulkers to fire on its attacker. And once damaged, the shulker may demonstrate its final trick: moving with alarming speed to a new location. Yes, the shulker might look passive, but it is a devilish opponent. And these blasted things don't even drop anything when they are killed. But adventurers wishing to raid End cities for their valuable treasures will need to face them nonetheless.

Fig. XXIX.

A shulker with shell open, shooting a projectile.

When closed, the shulker's shell might lead you to mistake it for a harmless purpur block.

The interior of the shell has a coiling pattern.

The shell opens periodically to search for intruders, revealing a small, fleshy head.

When a victim is sighted, the shulker fires a missile that seeks its target relentlessly.

Tapered abdomen gives a fish-like appearance.

Thorax appears to be covered in a furry substance.

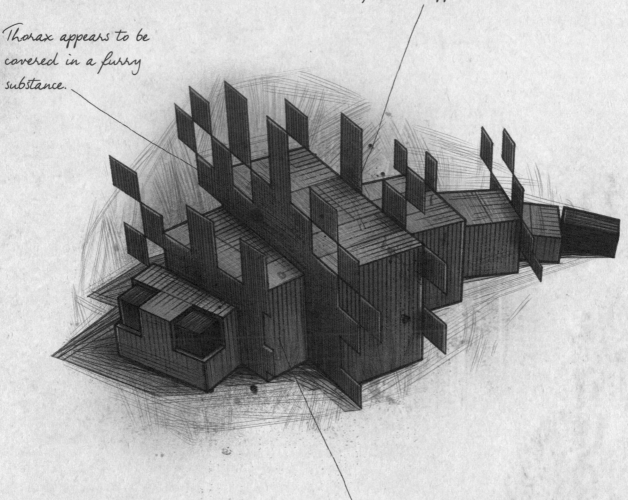

Being only half a slab in height, the silverfish finds sinking substances like soul sand to be fatal.

SILVERFISH

These scuttling little blighters swarm and chitter about one's feet, biting viciously. Despite their name, they are not fish but wingless insects with two bug eyes, a black-tipped tail and a dreadful furred body. In great numbers they present a serious threat to adventurers, and their infestations can cause great damage to buildings. They are a pest and a menace.

THE STONE DWELLER

Despite their foulness, scientists seem to find the silverfish fascinating. There are certainly no other mobs quite like the silverfish, and one grudgingly supposes that this makes them worthy of our attention.

The silverfish is one of the smallest mobs; second only to the positively minuscule endermite. But what makes them unique is where they live. Silverfish are not generally found wandering free in the Overworld. Rather, they are found living in strangely corrupted stone blocks called monster eggs. These blocks look like regular stone, whether common natural stone, or worked stone like chiseled, mossy, cracked or brick. But when they are broken by an unwary explorer, the creature bursts forth and bites the ankles of its liberator with vicious abandon.

Happily, monster eggs are rather rare. Explorers have reported that they are found in strongholds and igloos which have underground rooms, and are also very sparsely distributed in the wilds of extreme hills. This makes silverfish rare, too, although they can also be found emerging from monster spawners in strongholds.

HABITS OF SILVERFISH

If it finds itself without an adventurer to attack, a silverfish will head for a nearby stone block and burrow into it, transforming the block into a monster egg. Because a stronghold might be home to a silverfish monster spawner, any stone in those sinister underground structures may be infested. Anyone who decides to venture into a stronghold must exercise great caution.

When one silverfish is injured, all silverfish lurking in monster eggs nearby will leap out and join the attack. This can be catastrophic for an adventurer. While a lone silverfish can only issue a small bite, a horde of the things can together do mortal injury.

TACKLING THE PEST

So how might one deal with the silverfish? First, try not to disturb the stone of a stronghold so that you do not encounter silverfish in the first place. This is not always possible, particularly as a silverfish spawner might be present. In the case of encountering such a spawner, one's best first action is to brighten the room. Silverfish will not materialize if you place enough torches nearby.

Second, do not strike a silverfish unless you are sure you will kill it in a single blow, or you are ready to face a swarm. Many adventurers who take irritable swipes at a lone silverfish swiftly meet their downfall.

It is surprisingly difficult to kill a silverfish in one blow. Far more resilient than their size might suggest, they will endure even the blade of a diamond sword. It is therefore suggested that one drink a potion of strength which will ensure all who wield an iron sword or better will defeat a silverfish with every strike.

A silverfish is so small that when it crawls across soul sand, into which all mobs sink slightly, it will suffocate. This, quite frankly, serves these little inflictions right.

SKELETON

Many adventurers have fallen to the skeleton. But it is not yet understood how these undead creatures have risen, or who they were in life. Some have proposed that skeletons are ancient adventurers raised from death by an evil sorcerer. Others suggest they were given undeath by adventurers desecrating villager burial grounds. But all this is wild speculation.

HAUNTS OF THE SKELETON
Every adventurer has encountered a skeleton, whether at night on the open plains of the Overworld, in the fiery halls of the Nether, or while wandering dank caves. They fear sunlight and burn under its rays, but unlike zombies, they will attempt to seek shade or water to save themselves. Some say this suggests they possess surprising intelligence.

Skeletons fear wolves, which hunt them for their bones. Skeletons will run from them, but wolves will usually win the chase. Adventurers can take advantage of this by keeping a tame wolf as a companion. What inspires the skeleton's hatred for adventurers is less understood, particularly since skeletons do not attack villagers. They do, however, attack iron golems.

Not all skeletons are alike. Those which appear in the icy places of the world are called strays, the cold apparently preserving their tattered clothes. They behave similarly to their cousins other than in shooting arrows tipped with poison which causes slowness. Chronicles also record encounters with skeletons which carry swords and move faster than their bow-wielding siblings. Rarer still are those which have the intellect to pick up armor and weapons and use them. Note that those wearing helmets do not burn in sunlight.

BATTLE TACTICS
Skeletons can only withstand as much damage as a zombie, and may be defeated with just a few sword-strikes. But their bows make them a menace.

Researchers have found skeletons will notice enemies from 16 blocks away and then find a vantage point from which to shoot at a distance of about eight blocks, moving after loosing each arrow. Their accuracy depends on the world being explored; those in hard worlds are keen shots indeed. Each arrow does a varying amount of damage, but little more than a zombie's bite at its maximum. But if an adventurer has no bow, they can be hit with several arrows before they can reach striking distance with their sword. As such, the shield is of great use to those facing skeletons. Raising it will give protection from any missile fired at one's front. This will slow one's movements, but practiced warriors watch the skeleton closely and raise and lower their shields in time with its arrows.

Another favored tactic is to maneuver into a position that causes skeletons to shoot other creatures of the dark. For instance, if a skeleton should hit another skeleton, they will fight between themselves, creating a fine opportunity to flee or press the advantage.

SPOILS OF SKELETONS
Skeletons will drop up to two arrows and up to two bones when they die. Arrows are always useful, but the bone is a greatly useful item which tames wolves and crafts bonemeal to speed the growth of plants.

If a skeleton should deal the killing blow to a creeper, the creeper will drop a music disc. And if a charged creeper should kill a skeleton in its explosion, the skeleton will drop a skeleton mob head. This trophy can disguise its wearer so skeletons don't recognize it, allowing it to move closer without detection.

Fig. XXXI.

Field sketch of a skeleton wielding a bow alongside the uncommon sight of a skeleton wearing armor and wielding a sword.

Note the human bone structure – perhaps skeletons are ancient adventurers who were enslaved by some dark magic.

The skeleton is inclined to pick up armor which gives it protection from the sun.

A lack of muscle might make the skeleton weak, but when equipped with a bow they make dangerous opponents.

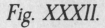

Fig. XXXII.

A formidable skeleton horseman that I happened upon during a particularly violent thunderstorm.

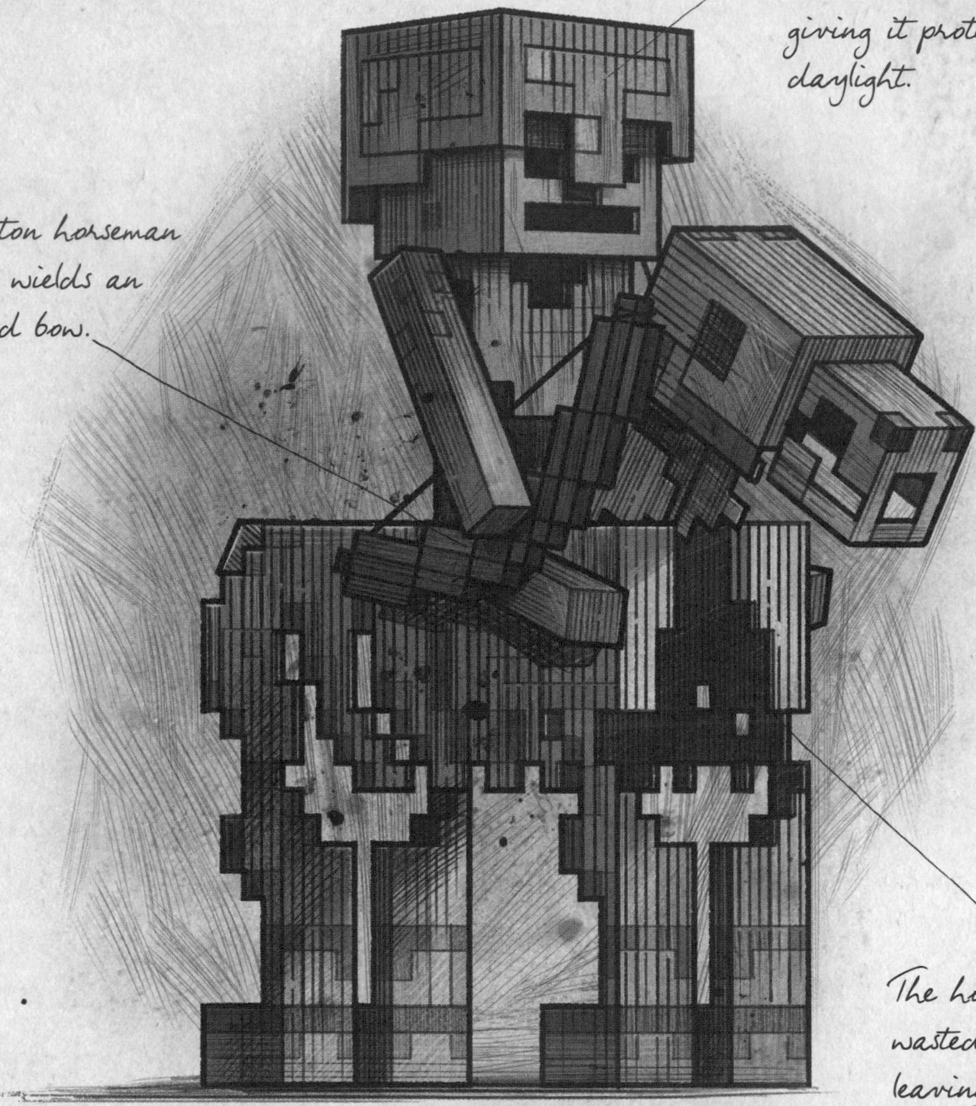

The horseman wears an enchanted iron helmet, giving it protection from daylight.

The skeleton horseman typically wields an enchanted bow.

The horse's flesh has wasted away entirely, leaving its skeleton exposed.

SKELETON HORSEMAN

Tales have long been told of skeletal riders, omens of the end of the world. Sighted by adventurers during storms, panic broke out as the news spread, and so scholars set out to discover whether the legends were true. Happily, we are now assured that skeleton horsemen are not a sign of the apocalypse. But they are nevertheless a fearsome phenomenon.

MANIFESTATION

The skeleton horseman comes into being as a result of a rare kind of lightning strike. The likelihood rises in accordance with the danger of the world, but most likely, only one in three lightning strikes will cause one to appear. At first, a skeleton horse will materialize and stand passively until an adventurer comes near, whereupon a second strike will flash and the horse will transform into four skeletal horses with skeleton riders wearing enchanted helmets and wielding enchanted bows.

For many adventurers, this is a good time to retreat. The riders' helmets prevent them from burning in the sun, so you are not safe by day. Thankfully, these horsemen do not haunt the land indefinitely. They will return to wherever they came from after fifteen minutes.

THE SKELETON RIDERS

In a similar manner to the spider jockey, the pairing moves swiftly. But unlike the spider jockey, the skeleton maintains full control over its mount, and thus behaves as it does when on foot, only at a greatly accelerated speed.

They will loose an arrow and move to avoid counterattacks before shooting again. They will find their favorite range from which to attack, moving away if one is to advance upon them, or closing the distance if one is far away.

The skeleton horseman will easily gallop out of range of a warrior attempting to attack it with a melee weapon. And one must remember that he has three comrades, who will often attempt to flank, a tactic that renders the shield, which will only defend one's front, quite ineffective.

A bow is, therefore, a better weapon. Many warriors swear by using an enchanted bow, perhaps infused with power, which increases the damage of its arrows. Very skilled warriors will also move in such a way as to encourage the riders to hit each other with their arrows, thereby causing them to fight one another. Any trick an adventurer can employ against these foes to make the battle easier is a good one. Consider also using the terrain to your advantage. Put a wall to your back so they cannot get behind you.

TAMING SKELETAL HORSES

As with all mounted mobs, the skeleton and the skeletal horse are quite separate creatures. If one is killed, the other will live on. Now, it was once assumed that the horse would harbor as much hatred for the living as its rider. But many warriors have reported that this is not true. If its rider is killed, the skeletal horses will placidly stand by.

In fact, the skeletal horse is tame, and seems quite happy to be ridden by any adventurer who does not mind taking such a morbid-looking steed. In fact, a great number of horse-loving adventurers see the inclusion of a skeletal horse in their stables as a mark of their skills as a wrangler. A saddle is required to control it, of course. It also looks rather uncomfortable to ride bareback, what with all those knobbly bones. What is more, other horses do not seem concerned by the presence of an undead member of their species in their midst, so one might quite easily integrate this nightmarish beast into one's herd.

SLIME

Do not allow the innocuous look of the slime to deceive you, as it can be the downfall of any wanderer of caverns and swamps. Slimes are apparently unrelated to any other Overworld inhabitant. (The Nether's magma cube seems likely to be a distant cousin.) They appear to obey their own laws and are therefore rather awkward to explain. But I shall try nonetheless.

NATURAL HABITAT

Slimes live underground and in swamps, and are found in three different sizes. Most students of the Overworld believe a slime's size reflects its age, yet adventurers have observed that their sizes are found in different proportions depending on the difficulty of the world being explored. Greater quantities of large slimes are found in worlds that are set to greater danger, while in easy ones they are more evenly distributed.

In swamps they tend to appear at night. One might assume that the hot sun would dry out their moist exterior, but they apparently feel no ill effects. There are, however, nights when slimes are more likely to be present. When the moon is full, I have observed that slimes seem to be common, and when it is new (when it is not illuminated), slimes mysteriously cannot be found. Scholars have suggested that they somehow require the moon's light.

Slimes shall appear underground without concern for light level. You might encounter them in chambers which explorers have already cleared of threats and lit with torches. And yet, slimes will not appear just anywhere under the earth. They seem to prefer certain areas, but science has uncovered no logic to why they favor one area over another. Advice to those wishing to establish truly safe passages would be to observe where slimes tend to appear and firmly block these sections off.

THE FIGHTING SLIME

If a slime becomes aware of an adventurer, it will bounce toward them to attack. They advance so eagerly that they will disregard such insignificant threats as cacti. Small and medium slimes will die in a single iron sword strike, and large ones fall in only three.

But the slime finds strength in numbers and speed. Research has shown that when a slime larger than the very smallest size is killed, it divides into between two and four new, smaller slimes. Thus, a large slime will divide into several medium slimes, and a medium slime will divide into several small ones. Unwary adventurers can therefore find themselves overwhelmed by a squelching horde.

In a single attack, a medium slime hurts less than a zombie bite and a large one does only a little more. But they are able to attack at twice the rate of other mobs. Thus, a crowd of slimes may deal considerable injury very quickly. One must take care never to be surrounded, and always keep the numbers one is facing under control. (Thankfully, small slimes are not capable of causing damage.)

DROPS

Slimes of medium size drop up to two slimeballs when killed, which can be crafted into several tools. Bouncy slime blocks provide entertainment and can safely cushion falls from high locations. Sticky pistons are vital for many machines. Leads are of great use to both farmers and owners of iron golems. And magma cream is a great aid for explorers of the Nether, since it produces the potion of fire resistance. The slime is a marvel indeed, but one would be wise not to underestimate it.

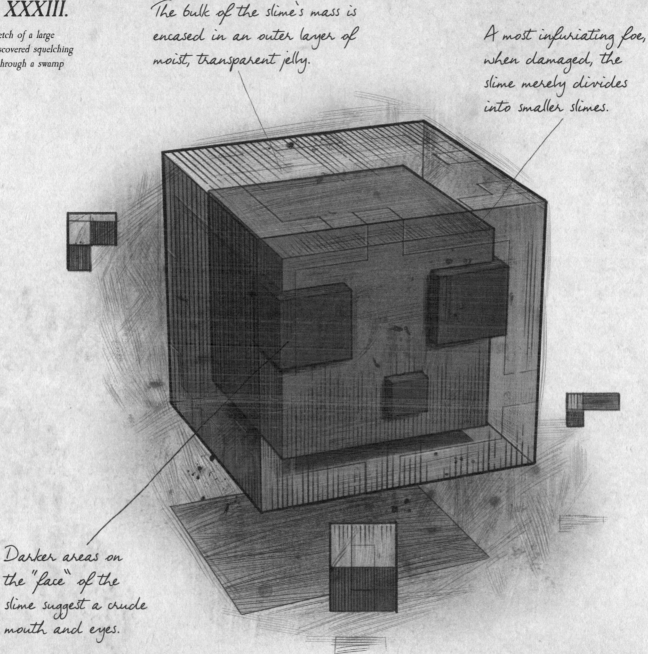

Fig. XXXIII.

Field sketch of a large
slime discovered squelching
its way through a swamp
biome.
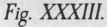

The bulk of the slime's mass is
encased in an outer layer of
moist, transparent jelly.

A most infuriating foe,
when damaged, the
slime merely divides
into smaller slimes.

Darker areas on
the "face" of the
slime suggest a crude
mouth and eyes.

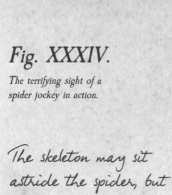

Fig. XXXIV.

The terrifying sight of a spider jockey in action.

The skeleton may sit astride the spider, but one should not assume it has control.

Being sat atop a rapidly scuttling monstrosity does not seem to reduce the accuracy of the skeleton's bow.

The spider's eight hairy legs vastly enhance the speed with which the skeleton might otherwise move.

SPIDER JOCKEY

The most dangerous pairing of mobs is that of the skeleton and the spider. The spider, so nimble and quick, and sitting astride its bulging abdomen a skeleton shooting deadly arrows. The combination of their skills and their hatred for adventurers is a threat to even the most experienced warrior. We have come to know this terrifying phenomenon as the spider jockey.

AN UNNATURAL UNION

Fortunately, the spider jockey is a rare occurrence. You might expect only to meet one spider with a skeleton rider among a hundred, and because the spider jockey is restricted to appearing in places where spiders are common, you will not come across one in the Nether through natural means. We must therefore be thankful that a wither skeleton cannot clamber onto a spider's hairy back. The combination of regular skeleton and spider is hazardous, however, for the two mobs attack separately, and thus can cause hurt at range and also close by.

The spider and skeleton are separate creatures, and they must both be killed in order to remove all threat. When one strikes the spider jockey, only one of the pair will be hit, leaving its mate to continue the assault when it dies.

SPIDER JOCKEY BEHAVIOR

For some time, it was assumed that the skeleton was master. But it has since been discovered that it is in fact the wily spider who reigns over the reins. By night, they act as one. The skeleton lends its tactical skill in flanking its victim, while the spider lends its speed and agility in climbing and leaping. In the same way one may be taken by surprise by a spider which has gained access to places thought to be safe, one might find a spider jockey scuttling up a wall and through one's open window.

By day, however, they are not quite such a happy pairing. The spider, turned passive as it naturally is during these hours, will ignore wandering adventurers, while its rider frantically fires arrows from its back. One can imagine the skeleton's frustration. Consider also that, being exposed to daylight, a skeleton without a helmet will also catch fire, but the spider will make no effort to find shade.

DEFEATING THE DUO

There are some reports of the skeleton killing its steed with badly aimed arrows. Chronicles have also recorded the spider scrambling into spaces the skeleton cannot fit and causing it to suffocate. They can, therefore, be a less than efficient team, but a wise warrior does not count on the spider jockey causing such problems for itself. At night, it is quite capable of seriously injuring the unwary.

Quick reactions and sturdy armor are one's best defense if taken by surprise. But if one is fortunate enough to spot a spider jockey at a distance, using a bow to keep it away is the best option. Ensure you focus your fire on either the spider or the skeleton so that their union will be quickly ended and one only has the other to contend with.

Do not expect great reward if you defeat a spider jockey. The spider will drop its usual string, the skeleton its usual bones and any armor it is wearing. The only real reward is the removal of the threat.

We can be thankful a wither skeleton has never been seen riding a cave spider. Oh, the combination of the cave spider's quickness and poison with the wither skeleton's terrible wasting disease...It would surely be one of the most deadly creatures of all the worlds.

VEX

This flying imp delights in causing ill toward explorers and villagers. Its name is appropriate: it is one of the most vexatious mobs one can encounter, and causes much mischief. Several vex are conjured at once by evokers in woodland mansions. How much control evokers have over their vex is a point of much debate, but it is clear that they are an evil pairing indeed.

CREATION OF THE VEX

Vex can only be created by an evoker and do not spawn on their own. The act of summoning is obvious, since it involves the evoker issuing white smoke from its outstretched arms while intoning a high chiming sound. Between two and four vexes will appear, hovering in the air around the creature, at which point they will begin to dart toward their unfortunate victim, hovering on their awful tattered wings and issuing breathy, low screams.

There appears to be no upper limit to the number of vex which an evoker can summon, and thus they would be able to develop into a malevolent cloud if it wasn't for the fact that their lifetime is limited. After between 30 and 100 or so seconds they will begin to take damage and die off. But the coast is not entirely clear until they disappear in clouds of noisome fumes.

FLYING DEVIL

Their height in the air gives them an overview of the room they are haunting, making it rather difficult to evade their attacks. Furthermore, they have the ability to pass through solid blocks, so constructing cover will not guarantee safety.

They cannot, however, see through blocks, so they will lose sight of their target if said target runs out of the chamber, slamming the door behind them. Once pacified in this way, the vex will return to its creator and hover about its head until its time in the Overworld comes to an end or another target presents itself.

Each vex wields an iron sword. They swoop toward their victims with a scream, and hit them with a force three times the power of a zombie bite. Having several of the things attacking at once, from all directions, will swiftly lead to the death of an unarmored adventurer.

Their bodies are tough and able to take a good deal of damage. They are also able to withstand heat from fire and lava without experiencing discomfort. I therefore urge all explorers of woodland mansions to exercise extreme caution, and to consider retreating to allow any summoned vexes to disappear before attempting a careful assault on their nefarious master, thus removing their threat at its source.

VEX BIOLOGY

We do not know what a vex's body is made from, since it has not yet been possible to obtain a specimen. But it is quite possible that it is not flesh as we know it. Reports show that its body exhibits two curious features. It issues a spectral light which does not illuminate its environment but does render the vex visible in the dark. Second is the sudden appearance of a strange crack of vivid red in its pale gray skin when it attacks.

Perhaps the interior of the vex is somehow composed of flame, a theory which might explain its resistance to heat. If so, perhaps the vex has some kind of demonic connection? Or perhaps they are artificial constructs of the evoker? If they are demonic, we have as yet discovered no evidence of vexes in the Nether. Much further study is required if we are to know this creature better!

Fig. XXXV.

Three vex in flight. Note that the vex at the top of the sketch is attacking, as indicated by the vivid red cracks in its skin.

The vex does not appear to be solid and has the ability to fly through blocks.

The vex's skin is an unnatural blue, and its eyes a ghostly white, suggesting the creature is undead.

A ghostly set of wings sprout from the vex's shoulders.

Fig. XXXVI.

An axe-wielding vindicator discovered inside a woodland mansion.

A clear relation to the evoker, the vindicator has the same unnatural gray skin.

The vindicator wields its axe in a menacing gesture.

The vindicator favors a short jacket and striped trousers rather than a robe.

VINDICATOR

Like the evoker, the vindicator was expelled from villages for its unspeakable activities, and it too wanders the halls of the eerie woodland mansions. Vindicators are more common than evokers, and have a disturbing love of violence and destruction. We do not know what they are trying to achieve out there in the woods, but we must all be on our guard.

BEWARE THE AXEMAN

Vindicators are found in rooms in woodland mansions, either alone, with up to two others of their kind, or in a pair with an evoker to lead them. Other than their sickly gray skin, they appear like an ordinary villager, but they dress smartly, wearing a black jacket and dark green trousers.

As an illager, their numbers in the world are limited. They do not breed or reproduce in any way, and once they are discovered they will remain present in that place until they are defeated.

Vindicators are extremely hostile. If they should spy an adventurer, villager or iron golem, they will uncross their arms to reveal their axe and rush at speed toward their target, chopping at them in a frenzied manner.

Our axes are fit only for chopping wood and are of little utility as a weapon. The vindicators' axes are honed for war, however. Some are even enchanted; the vindicators wield them with terrifying strength. They deliver blows of brutality which know few equals across the known worlds, and their thirst for battle is strong. Little will stop them once they have a target in their sights.

SAVAGE TACTICS

Little, that is, except for an experienced adventurer such as you or I. With care and skill, these brutes can be put in their place. First, armor or protective enchantments are necessary to reduce the impact of their crushing strikes. Reports also suggest it is best to engage vindicators on one's own terms, so never attempt to face a group of them in an open space, where they might surround one. Make a tactical retreat to a doorway or similar opening so they might be faced one at a time.

Facing two vindicators and an evoker at once can be too much. Remember that as well as avoiding the vindicators' axes, one will be watching for the evoker's fangs and its summoning of vexes. A single adventurer, even one greatly skilled, can easily be overpowered by their collective onslaught. Consider bringing companions, whether other adventurers or such protectors as iron golems. The golem's sheer toughness will see it survive a vindicator's attention for some time, but do not think of them as impervious: in a world of normal difficulty it will only take eight of the vindicator's devastating strikes before the golem falls.

Do not attempt to be a hero against such a powerful foe. The vindicator is stupid enough to forget all about its intended victim after a short time, and there is no honor lost in running away if it means one can survive.

FELLING THE VINDICATOR

While a vindicator hits with great violence, it is not overly robust in terms of its body: it is only a little tougher than a zombie. On death it may drop up to one emerald and has a small chance of dropping its axe.

I have heard stories of a particularly violent vindicator called, of all things, Johnny. This individual is apparently so blood-crazed that it will attack any mob nearby, except evokers and other vindicators. The stories say that Johnny was driven to this state by too much work and too little play.

WITCH

The witch cackles with glee and hurls foul potions at any explorer who has the misfortune to cross it. Are they village outcasts, chased away for playing with forces they shouldn't? Or do they choose to live apart? Whichever is the case, one must not drop one's guard if, when wandering a swamp, dark cavern or glade, one should encounter a humanoid figure.

HABITS OF WITCHES

Witches practice their sorcery in small huts elevated on stilts above the murky waters of swamps. Inside, one will find witches' tools: a crafting table, cauldron and a plant pot in which they grow herbs to use in their brews.

It is fairly rare to encounter such huts, but witches wander far and wide at night and in dark areas. One should always listen for their screeches. Occasionally, witches may also be seen in villages, especially after storms. I did not understand why until I witnessed a villager struck by lightning, transforming it into a witch. Perhaps this is their origin.

Though some wonder if witches are rejected by villagers because of their evil intents, there is no evidence they attack villagers. However, they are also peaceful with malevolent mobs, so do not think them innocent.

FOUL MAGIC

Witches use potions to attack enemies and defend themselves, employing their knowledge of these concoctions. First,

they will usually try to slow their foe with a potion of slowness to prevent their retreat. Then, they will throw a potion of poison to sap the life from all in the immediate vicinity. It can be hard to get close to the crone, but those who do will more than likely find themselves under assault from potions of weakness, which reduce the power of their offensive strikes.

It is quite usual to be afflicted by all three of these effects at once. If this is the case, the witch will begin throwing potions of harming at you, which can prove to be fatal if one is already weakened by poison. The witch will also drink potions to heal injuries and ailments, and increase their speed so as to stay in range of their victim. They also have an uncanny knack of adapting to afflictions or environmental circumstances. If one should set the witch on fire, it will take fire resistance. If in water, it will take water breathing.

Warriors who have attempted to use potions against witches have recorded that they shrug off their effects. One weakness of the witch is that it will

attack another witch if caught by its splash potions. Chronicles record them struggling against each other for hours, neither able to get the upper hand, such is their resilience to magic.

DEFEATING THE WITCH

To answer the witch's trickery, one must resort to simple weapons, but some warriors also take a potion of speed to counteract their potions of slowness, and regeneration to prevent the harm of poison. Many prefer using a bow, so they might attack from range, but a good sword will do, too. Attack without mercy, and the witch will soon fall; its healing potions cannot keep up with a constant flurry of blows.

Fortunately, the rewards for killing these loathsome figures are excellent. They hide many items in the folds of their robes, such as glass bottles, glowstone dust, gunpowder, redstone, spider eyes, sugar and sticks, and will leave an assortment of six behind. If they happen to be drinking a potion at the moment of their death, then they may drop that, too.

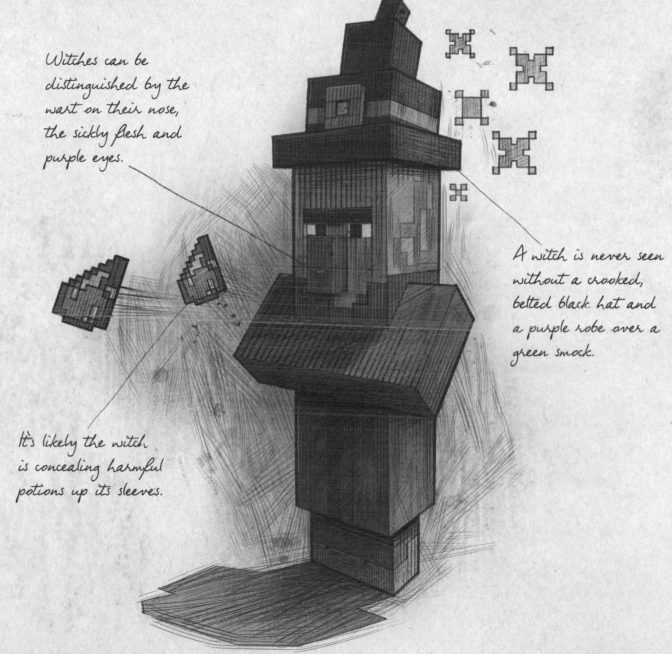

Fig. XXXVII.

Field sketch of a witch attacking an adventurer with foul potions.

Witches can be distinguished by the wart on their nose, the sickly flesh and purple eyes.

A witch is never seen without a crooked, belted black hat and a purple robe over a green smock.

It's likely the witch is concealing harmful potions up its sleeves.

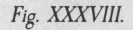

Fig. XXXVIII.

The imposing figure of a wither skeleton as it patrols a Nether fortress.

Standing an impressive 2.4 blocks tall, the wither skeleton uses its formidable stature to intimidate.

The wither skeleton uses its stone sword to inflict damage.

Its bones are charred black, as if they have been scoured by fire.

WITHER SKELETON

This imposing creature of the Nether concerns even the most experienced warriors. Its towering form begs many questions: What kind of creature was it when it was alive? Did they build the Nether fortresses? They stand tall and are fearless and strong, their bones charred black, but it is their ability to cause a wasting disease known simply as "wither" which causes great fear.

FORTRESS DWELLER

It is often suggested that the wither skeleton is some form of officer or leader among its weaker skeletal cousins. Brave statisticians have found that if one should find ten skeletons, eight of them will be wither skeletons, and only two regular skeletons.

Thankfully, the wither skeleton has a weakness. While the fire-loving creatures of the Nether have no fear of light, the wither skeleton will only appear where it is dark. One might use torches to discourage its presence.

DANGERS OF WITHER

A wither skeleton wields its sword with surprising strength given its spindly arms. To be struck by it causes great injury, but this is only the beginning of its victim's slow death.

Few who have been infected by wither have returned to tell of it, but we have nevertheless gained a reasonable understanding. It is a disease which turns its sufferers' hearts black, and causes their health to steadily reduce every two seconds. It acts a little like poison, but with one crucial difference: while poison will not kill, merely leaving you close to death, wither will eventually consume one entirely.

When the wither effect was first encountered, we immediately set out to find a cure. Two possible ways to counter it were discovered. First, a potion of regeneration will restore health faster than wither will leach it. But it will not remove the wither effect. For this, one needs milk. Anyone who plans to visit a Nether fortress would do well to take as many buckets of the stuff as they can carry.

When facing the wither skeleton, I suggest that warriors enchant their weapons with the smite enchantment, a magic that causes greater damage to all the undead, including wither skeletons. One might also use the wither skeleton's height against it. Standing at a little over two blocks tall, it cannot walk through doorways which are under three blocks in height. In this way, one might control the wither skeleton's access to spaces by creating low doorways which one may easily enter, but will leave wither skeletons standing, quite helpless, on the other side.

THE WITHER SKULL

The wither skeleton is of particular interest to adventurers like us because of its skull. Three of them are required to resurrect the wither, a terrible creature which must be killed to gain the fabulously precious Nether star. You will find extensive notes on this item later in these pages.

To find a wither skeleton's skull is rare. Far more commonly, they merely leave coal and bones behind. Studies have examined the frequency with which the wither skull might be found, concluding that if one were to kill 40 wither skeletons, one can expect to find a single skull. Looting enchantments will help, but one must still expect to have to kill many wither skeletons before succeeding.

My message to adventurers is not to give up the quest. Grip your sword, and step forth once again. With bravery comes victory.

ZOMBIE

The zombie is the commonest of all the mobs that wish to do us harm, but most seasoned adventurers do not see them as a serious threat, since they are slow and announce their presence with loud groans. Yet scientists now agree that most zombies are us, or were us. It is not a pleasant idea to consider, but one can see the similarities in their tattered clothes and shape.

THE ZOMBIE POPULATION

Zombies can usually be found wandering aimlessly in groups of four, anywhere in the Overworld by night, and also any area of darkness underground. They will sometimes wear armor and wield weapons; very occasionally they may even be diamond and enchanted.

In sunlight, most zombies will burn, unless they are wearing helmets, but "husks," which are found in deserts, do not, and also inflict hunger on their victims. One in twenty zombies is a baby zombie, a miniature terror which hurtles about the world by both night and day. It even hijacks chickens to ride them as the chicken jockey. Another one in twenty zombies will clearly once have been a villager.

When this phenomenon was first observed, researchers were confused. How were villagers becoming zombies? We then heard the first reports of zombies' mass midnight attacks on villages. Such is the size of some of these hordes, even villages' iron golems may fall. The zombies pursue the villagers and take to pounding on their doors, and may sometimes succeed in breaking through. (Only iron doors will hold firm against zombies, though they can reach through even these.)

Those villagers caught by the zombies are often transformed into zombie villagers. But one can cure them through a process you will find detailed in this book's entry for the villager. It is a difficult process, and only works on zombie villagers, but it has led some to wonder whether all zombification might somehow be reversed. Moreover, why do zombies hate villagers with such vehemency? Perhaps to swell their numbers with new zombies?

SHAMBLERS' HABITS

It is easy to dismiss zombies as being slow and dim, but they have some surprising abilities. They have the unparalleled capacity to sense their prey, perceiving adventurers and villagers from some forty blocks away. They cannot smell adventurers, so by keeping out of sight behind a wall, one can remain undetected. Villagers are not so lucky, however. Perhaps they are more pungent?

Zombies can also work as a group. They may call nearby zombies into attacks against adventurers. In hard worlds some leader zombies can even summon comrades to appear. If we should ever decode their grunts and groans, we may understand some kind of language, as unattractive as the idea of talking to zombies might seem.

ZOMBIE HUNTING

Zombies are not quick, but their bites can hurt a good deal. One should take care to avoid being bitten when zombies are burning in daylight, because they may set one on fire, too. But they are most dangerous in crowds. In these situations, one must stay calm and strike with a sword's sweep attack to keep them back.

Because zombies are undead, they will not be hurt by potions of harming. They fear healing potions, however, and so in close combat one can throw splash potions at their feet, thus healing yourself and damaging nearby zombies in a single act. It is an effective technique and excellent against skeletons, too.

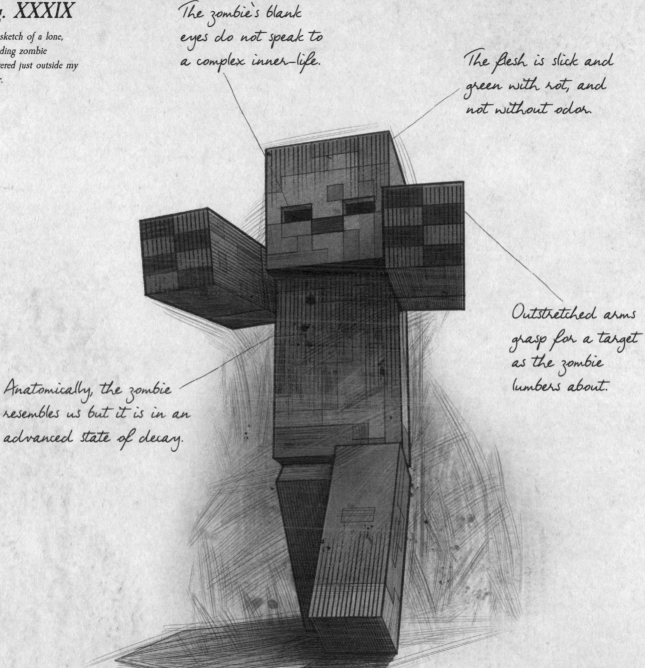

Fig. XXXIX

Early sketch of a lone,
marauding zombie
discovered just outside my
shelter.

The zombie's blank
eyes do not speak to
a complex inner-life.

The flesh is slick and
green with rot, and
not without odor.

Outstretched arms
grasp for a target
as the zombie
lumbers about.

Anatomically, the zombie
resembles us but it is in an
advanced state of decay.

TAMEABLE MOBS

There are some mobs which, if one can capture
and tame them, will be of great use to any adventurer.
In the following pages you will find detailed accounts
of how to tame these creatures.

Fig. XL.

A herd of horses discovered in a plains biome. Note that it includes the rare, tamed skeleton variant.

Seven variant coats have been spotted. Each may have distinctive markings, or none at all.

Stockily built, the horse's powerful back easily bears the weight of an adventurer.

HORSE

The horse proudly roams the open plains and savannas of the Overworld in herds of between two and six. With this nobility comes a certain strength of character which can cause the horse to be a handful to control. One can become a horse's partner, but never truly its master. Yet it will repay one with advantages the likes of which all adventurers will find useful.

TAMING THE HORSE

Taming a horse is not straightforward. Gaining a horse's respect is dependent upon its attitude. Each horse has a certain temper which makes it more or less likely to accept someone riding it.

One's first attempt at riding a horse usually ends in one being bucked off. But with every try, the horse will soften its opinion, though one may also even the odds by feeding the horse its favorite foods. Sugar, wheat and apples seem to improve its temperament a little, but greater effect may be achieved with a golden carrot, or, best of all, a golden apple, which horses adore.

USES OF HORSES

Once tamed, a horse may be ridden freely. But one needs a saddle in order to exercise control. Saddles are a rather rare item which may be found in chests in such places as blacksmiths' houses, dungeons and Nether fortresses, or you may be able to trade for one with villagers. One might want to spend some time selecting a suitable horse before setting out on a long ride, since each horse differs in its abilities. Some explorers favor speed. The fastest horses may travel up to three times one's walking speed. Imbuing one's horse with potions of speed will cause it to gallop still faster. Others may favor a horse's jumping ability. They may be compelled to leap surprising heights and distances, sometimes twice that of a person.

And some warriors, who like to swing their swords from horseback, favor a horse's health. One might equip one's steed with horse armor to make it even more resilient, but it is advised to keep a stock of food to maintain its condition. Hay bales are remarkably effective for this purpose.

A brief note: in the sad event of a horse dying, it will drop up to two leather and anything it may be carrying.

The Overworld is not only home to horses but also to their smaller cousin, the donkey. Donkeys do not stand so tall and haughty as horses, but they do provide their own very special service to those they respect. Instead of wearing armor, they will consent to carry a good number of items. They may, therefore, be employed as mobile chests, allowing one to transport many goods easily over long distances.

BREEDING HORSES

Only the golden carrot or apple will induce horses to breed. Their foal will be born untamed, and so will need to be broken in, in order to ride. Breeding two horses together will result in a horse foal, and two donkeys will lead to a young donkey. But breeding a horse and a donkey together will birth a separate subspecies, the mule, which has the long ears and behavior of a donkey (and thus shares its ability to carry items) but has a darker coat and almost reaches the size of the horse.

There are two forms of horse that are rather less noble than the others. The skeleton horse is discussed elsewhere, but it has been rumored that there exists another such terrible creature: the zombie horse. Scholars have recently discovered that the tales seem to be regrettably true, though the creature is only conjured through the most unnatural of means.

LLAMA

The llama's natural homes are the plateau savanna and the mountainous extreme hills. As such, they are hardy beasts that thrive in dry heat and bitingly cold outcrops alike. They are also delightfully amiable, and content to loyally accompany any adventurer. Once tamed, they will perform many useful tasks, becoming a valuable member of any wilderness expedition.

MOUNTAIN MAMMAL

Llamas are grazing animals and are generally found in groups of four or five, sometimes with young. They seem to prefer being at the top of the inclines and hills in their natural environments, and as such are best understood as creatures of the mountains. They are accordingly strong and kept warm by their woolly coats, which come in four different colors: a shaggy brown, a sandy yellow, a mottled gray and white.

They are docile beasts unless provoked, whether by explorer or most mobs. But if they should feel attacked, they will spit at their aggressor just once, lobbing a gob of saliva with such speed that it actually does a small amount of damage. Llamas do not need provocation to spit at wild wolves, however. Researchers have observed fierce wolves fleeing as a result of a herd of llamas' efforts.

USES OF THE LLAMA

Once tamed, these woolly creatures boast many characteristics which are of great utility to explorers. They are domesticated in a similar manner to horses, which is to say that one attempts to mount one's chosen beast several times. It is not, however, advised that one rides a llama. They take an adventurer's weight and do not buck, but refuse to obey any command.

But do not assume the llama is obstinate. With the help of a lead they will become obedient indeed. Use the device, which is crafted with string and a slimeball, on a single animal and up to nine nearby llamas, both tamed and wild, adult and baby, will form behind it in a caravan. They will then follow their leader, keeping up even if one sets a sprinting pace, but do take care on particularly treacherous ground.

A caravan of llamas is a fantastic sight. But this train of beasts is more than simply a curiosity. Each llama can be equipped with a chest and thus perform as a wonderful pack animal, ready to haul one's goods across the Overworld. You will see the chest slung across the beast's back and it will contain a varying number of items, from three to fifteen, depending on the animal's strength. One might wish to try out several animals for suitability before choosing the members of one's caravan to ensure maximum carrying capacity.

A DECORATIVE BEAST

To give one's caravan a celebratory air, one can have the llamas wear colorful cloths instead of a chest. Use colored wool on them and one will see a delicately patterned piece of it draped over their backs and around their necks and heads.

Like any other domesticated animal, llamas can be bred. Give two adults hay bales to induce them to breed and they will produce a baby llama. It will sport the woolly coat of one of its parents, and its strength will be influenced by its parents, though many llama breeders report that even two of the strongest llamas cannot always produce strong offspring. If one wishes to breed a strong caravan, one must be prepared to work hard. To close on this delightful and useful mob, llamas drop up to two leather on their sad death, but one mustn't let them fall to such a fate. Please look after these beasts of burden.

Pronounced snout aids powerful spitting — the llama's only defense mechanism.

The llama's long neck and strong back lend themselves to the transportation of items.

Woolly coat keeps the llama warm.

Fig. XLII.

Sketch of a wild ocelot with two tame cats.

The tamed cat is smaller in size than the wild ocelot.

Spotted coat helps the ocelot to remain camouflaged in the jungle's dappled light.

A long tail aids balance when the ocelot is leaping through the jungle trees.

OCELOT

It is often said that one is either a wolf person or an ocelot person, but both creatures offer excellent companionship. In biological terms, the ocelot is a wild creature of the jungle, and transforms into a cat when it is tamed. Both these beasts will be examined here but to avoid confusion, from here on we shall refer to the two forms of this feline by their proper names.

THE WILD OCELOT

The ocelot roams the undergrowth of jungles as a masterful hunter of the chicken. It will crawl, low to the ground, until it is within range of its clucking prey, and then it will pounce with heartstoppingly lethal grace. One can't help but feel for the unlucky chicken, but such is the circle of life.

Ocelots are afraid of adventurers, and will bolt at the sight of them. (Ocelots and cats are one of the few mobs which are known to be able to sprint.) Indeed, ocelots also appear to have heightened senses, which may perceive an adventurer even if they have taken a potion of invisibility. They may also fall from any height without being hurt.

TAMING THE OCELOT

One can persuade an ocelot to overcome its fear of adventurers by taking advantage of its love for raw fish. Hold some near an ocelot and it will cautiously inch closer until one can feed it. Do not move. It is awfully easy to scare it away. Be patient, and one might be lucky that the act of feeding will tame the creature.

It is quite clear when one has been successful. The ocelot will immediately transform, becoming smaller and taking one of three types of fur: black and white, tabby, or a tan-colored Siamese. If one is unsuccessful in one's attempt to tame it, the ocelot will still show its pleasure and will be induced to breed, which, if one feeds another nearby ocelot, will result in offspring.

CAT OWNERSHIP

The cat is a delightful companion, purring, meowing and following one about. But the cat can be somewhat headstrong, unreliable, and sometimes quite maddening when one has urgent tasks to perform.

If a cat should venture close to a warm and comfortable place, namely chests, beds or working furnaces, it is likely to hop up onto it and sit, rendering the blocks quite inaccessible until it leaves. It will ignore all commands to get down, but can be enticed with some fish or pushed off. This vexing habit has driven some settlers to enclose their utilities so their cats cannot gain access to them. They do not seem to enjoy being ordered to perform tasks very much, but in the event that one sets out for a quest, one can encourage a cat to stay at home by commanding it to sit. They are, after all, lazy creatures.

To be quite truthful, cats have few truly practical uses, unlike the wolf, which will loyally hurl itself into battle alongside its master. But cats have one property which may save one's life. The cat and ocelot cause creepers such fear that they run away at the sight of them. Scholars have found no reason for this terror, especially since cats seem to entirely ignore these explosive scoundrels.

A wise adventurer might therefore use cats as creeper deterrents, but a wiser one will never assume they are entirely safe. Cats will not actively chase creepers, and so creepers may find their way through one's feline defenses. Oh, if only cats would work a little harder. They are rather exasperating, but when one hears their homely meows, one cannot help but forgive them everything.

WOLF

Overworld life can indeed be hard and dispiriting, but one can find comradeship even in the most isolated of places. Arguably the best choice of companion is the wolf. One might think the wolf too wild a beast to become a friend, but it takes little effort to tame. Once tamed, the wolf will become not only a grateful companion but also a faithful protector.

HABITAT OF WILD WOLVES

Wolves are creatures of forests and taiga, their thick fur providing warmth against the cold. They are found in packs of four, sometimes with pups, and hunt rabbits and sheep. Their ability to work as a pack is quite remarkable. Folk stories so often take great pleasure in painting this proud animal as a bloodthirsty killer, but the truth is that in the Overworld the wild wolf will not attack an adventurer unless it is provoked.

An angered wolf is a fierce sight, its eyes inflamed and tail outstretched, and it attacks with great leaps. For a seasoned warrior, a single wolf is not a great threat, falling to two sweeps of a sword. But being loyal animals, to attack one wolf is to attack its entire pack, and all wolves across a wide area will retaliate. But since they drop no items, there is no need to attack them.

TAMING THE WOLF

Taming wolves is quite straightforward. All one needs to do is to give them bones; it may take several bones before the wolf is satisfied. (Take care not to accidentally hit the wolf with the bone. The creature will think itself attacked.) A tamed wolf may be identified by its red-colored collar, amiable eyes and raised tail, and it will follow its master everywhere unless ordered to sit. It is a fearless and loyal companion, and will attack almost anything which assaults its master, even other adventurers, and most mobs that its master attacks, too.

LIVING WITH WOLVES

A tamed wolf is not slow-witted, and it will not attempt to attack creepers or ghasts which might lead to its doom. As such, one does not need to avoid danger. But, sadly, it is bound to be injured sooner or later. Though a tamed wolf is tougher than a wild one (one can assess its health by the height of its tail), a good master will feed it meat to restore its energy. Wolves are not picky eaters: rotten flesh will do.

A tamed wolf will not hunt for rabbits and sheep, but it will still viciously attack skeletons without a second thought. It is therefore an excellent partner for all kinds of journeys, keeping one safe without need for commands. Indeed, wolves have an uncanny ability to keep up with their masters if they have not been ordered to sit. But they are not indestructible. Some explorers have written sad accounts of journeys on which they have found their wolves falling from heights as they attempt to follow them.

One might wish to keep several tamed wolves in case one is lost. Finding new wild wolves to tame can be troublesome, but tame wolves may be bred by feeding a pair meat when they are fully healthy. Their puppy will have the same master as its parents. (If its two parents have different masters, then the puppy's master will be that of the parent that was most recently tamed.)

An owner might wish to distinguish their wolves from other wolves. One can use dye to color their collar, or one can use a name tag. As a closing point, there is a belief that if one's pet should die, all adventurers exploring a world at the time will become inexplicably aware.

Fig. XLIII.

*Field sketch of a hostile wolf
alongside two tamed wolves.
Note the distinction between
the eyes and tail position.*

Mottled, pale fur helps the
wolf slip unseen through
the snowy landscape.

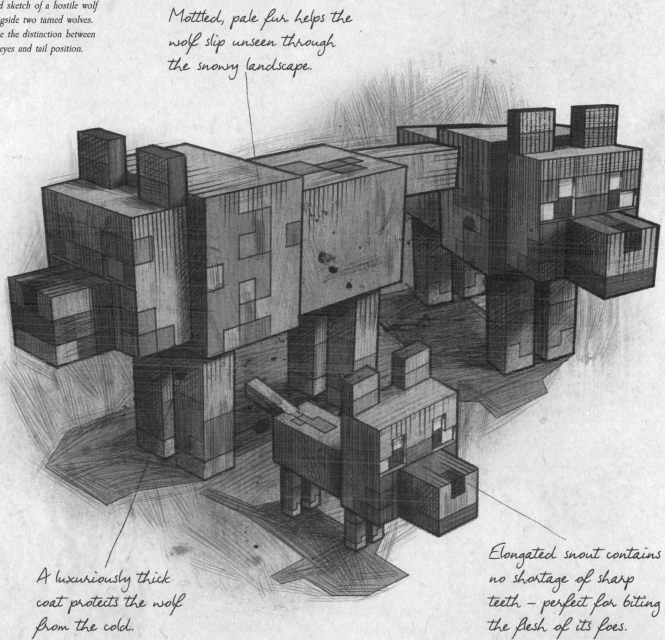

A luxuriously thick
coat protects the wolf
from the cold.

Elongated snout contains
no shortage of sharp
teeth – perfect for biting
the flesh of its foes.

BOSS MOBS

Dare you read on?
The following entries concern the most formidable creatures
I have yet encountered. These boss mobs have unnatural
powers, but, if one can defeat them, one will
be rewarded with valuable treasures.

Fig. XLIV.

*The terrifying depiction of a
wither in attack mode.*

Each head turns independently
to fire wither skulls, inflicting
the wither effect on their target.

The wither's three
fleshless heads are those
of wither skeletons.

Its trio of skulls converge
onto a black spine and
an empty ribcage, ending
in a curved tailbone.

THE WITHER

Huge, vicious and terrible, the wither kills without hesitation and causes disease and destruction wherever it goes. Its existence was theorized by scholars before it was witnessed. Soon after, a bizarre painting began to appear, showing a T-shaped group of brownish blocks topped by three white-eyed heads. Thus the search began for information as to what this creature may be.

SUMMONING THE WITHER

There is something to be said about the curiosity of explorers that leads them to try anything, even if it ends in their doom. A group of settlers tried to re-create what they saw in that painting, using four blocks of soul sand and three skulls of the wither skeleton. They found terrible success. With a scream and a burst of fumes, a glowing monstrosity appeared before them. All was quiet for a few moments, until it let forth an almighty explosion. And so the battle had begun.

It seems a cruel joke that one is forced to summon the wither, but it is the only means of obtaining a Nether star, which is necessary to craft the beacon.

THE WITHER ASSAULT

Directly after appearing, the wither will steadily grow, its body pulsing with blue light. Impervious to all attacks at this time, it is gathering its strength in order to unleash the most powerful explosion in the world. Thus warriors must retreat at least ten blocks, or prepare adequate defense, to avoid it. After detonation, the wither will begin its attack. Its hatred for life is so intense that it will attack not only brave adventurers who summon it, but also any mob which is not undead. The wither can smash blocks that lie in its way, and even obsidian will crumble. Only bedrock and End portal blocks can withstand it.

Let us consider its three heads. They behave independently and allow the wither to assault three foes at once, shooting wither skulls at their targets. The blast of these explosive projectiles does not extend more than a block or two, but they do a good deal of injury. More dangerously, however, they cause wither, a wasting disease which turns one's heart black and steadily reduces one's health until one is dead. And the disease somehow uses one's vigor to restore the wither's own health.

THE ROAD TO VICTORY

When one finally injures the wither enough to reduce it to half health, it conjures spectral armor which makes arrows and potions useless against it. This point of the battle offers one cause for hope, however. Its glowing protection appears to weigh it down, so it can no longer hover high out of the reach of one's sword.

There are many ways to fight the wither. Some use trickery, summoning it in such a place that it suffocates in bedrock. But I suggest a more sensible one. Take a strong bow for the first half of the battle, when it flies high. Put on your diamond armor and enchant it with protection, which prevents one from becoming diseased, and carry a diamond sword with smite to increase damage against this undead horror. Have ready potions of health and strength, and golden apples.

There is much to make ready. Choose an open space in which to summon it, and then run back before it explodes. Keep it at a distance while firing with a bow. Some suggest bringing wolves and golems into the fight. They can certainly distract it, but they will also be struck down with wither, thereby restoring the wither's health. When the wither drops to the ground, leap in with your sword. The clash will be long, but the reward is great.

THE ENDER DRAGON

One can only imagine the panic that those first explorers felt when they encountered this dark lizard and realized it stood between them and their homes. In the years since, many warriors have returned victorious from the End, bringing with them tales of their experiences. Arm yourself with all they learned, and you too will be ready to follow in their footsteps.

POWER OF THE DRAGON

The ender dragon is found in the dark of the End, circling high above a ring of obsidian towers. It is elegant in flight and utterly terrifying. It attacks its foes with great bites, buffets them with beats of its wings, and bombards them with exploding fireballs which release spurts of purple acid that linger and burn. The scaly hide that covers its vast body is the toughest of any mob we know, able to absorb countless blows. Only its head takes full damage. And it is healed by the ender crystals on each of the towers.

It is of little wonder that the endermen which cluster on the grounds below seem to worship this beast. One cannot help feeling similar admiration.

WEAPONS OF CHOICE

The ender dragon flies far outside the range of any melee weapon, so bringing a bow to the End is of great importance, along with many arrows. Consider enchanting it with power. Then, a strong sword is needed for when the dragon is within reach. Armor capable of resisting its terrible attacks is also essential. Furthermore, enchanting this armor with protection will be greatly beneficial. Finally, one needs as much food and potions of healing and regeneration as one can carry to keep one's strength up.

Fighting the ender dragon is not a case of merely attacking. One must solve two tricky problems. First, the dragon must be prevented from regenerating its health by destroying the ender crystals atop each tower. Climbing up to the crystals is exceedingly dangerous, since one is exposed to being knocked off by the dragon's wings. Thus, shooting them from the ground is the best strategy; watch for the explosion marking their destruction. But some crystals are enclosed in iron cages. Decide carefully whether climbing up to these crystals is worth the risk.

Secondly, one must consider the crowds of endermen, for you are likely to catch their gaze during the battle. One can wear a pumpkin on one's head to prevent this, but remember that it restricts your view and provides rather less protection than a helmet.

THE ULTIMATE VICTORY

Once enough crystals are destroyed, the battle begins in earnest. Shoot ahead of the dragon in order to land a hit on it. Expect it to fly down and discharge its fireballs or bite, and, if one is close to the portal in the middle of the area, it will breathe purple acid. Yet there is hope. Strike when it presents openings and keep moving to avoid its attacks. Expect a long battle, but with care and patience, victory will be yours.

When the ender dragon is slain, the portal to the Overworld opens and its egg appears. The dragon egg only appears once, and may only be picked up if it falls onto such blocks as torches or signs. But if it falls on solid ground, it will break forever. One method is to cause it to fall by mining under it, but it is first found resting on impervious bedrock. Attacking it causes it to teleport, one hopes, to a place it may be mined. Even in death the dragon presents its challengers with trials! But for those skilled enough to collect it, its egg is a trophy of the rarest glory.

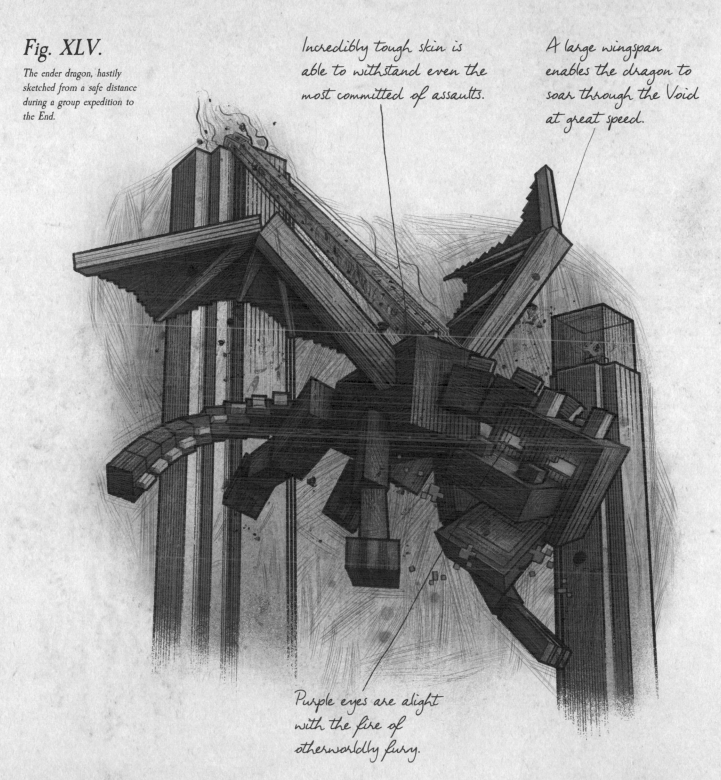

Fig. XLV.

The ender dragon, hastily sketched from a safe distance during a group expedition to the End.

Incredibly tough skin is able to withstand even the most committed of assaults.

A large wingspan enables the dragon to soar through the Void at great speed.

Purple eyes are alight with the fire of otherworldly fury.